Into the Depths

A Journey of Loss and Vocation

-<-<--►->-

MARY MARGARET FUNK

-<-<--►->-

Lantern Books ● New York

A Division of Booklight Inc.

2011

LANTERN BOOKS
128 Second Place
Brooklyn, NY 11231
www.lanternbooks.com

All Biblical quotations are taken from the New Revised Standard of the Bible (Nashville: Thomas Nelson, 1989)

Library of Congress Cataloging-in-Publication Data

Funk, Mary Margaret.
Into the depths : a journey of loss and vocation / Mary Margaret Funk.
p. cm.
ISBN-13: 978-1-59056-235-2 (alk. paper)
ISBN-10: 1-59056-235-6 (alk. paper)
1. Funk, Mary Margaret. 2. Missionaries—Bolivia—Biography. 3. Accidents—Religious aspects—Christianity. 4. Loss (Psychology)—Religious aspects—Christianity. 5. Consolation. I. Title.
BV2853.B5F86 2010
266'.2092—dc22
[B]
2010030087

Into the Depths

To all the Juanitos in the world, and those who care for them

The fear of the Lord is the beginning of wisdom.

—Proverbs 1:7

Contents

Acknowledgments

This book would not have come about without the use of a transcription of a talk I gave to a group of Cistercian nuns one December evening around the wood-burning stove in the office of Abbess Marie Fahy of St. Mary's Abbey in Glencairn, Co. Waterford, Ireland. The nuns had the capacity to listen deeply to the story that this book contains, and I'm indebted to their profound attention. *Into the Depths* would also not have been possible without the commitment and thoughtfulness of Martin Rowe, who had the patience to wait nearly ten years until I was ready to tell the story in full, and who allowed me to do it in my own time and in my own way.

I'm also grateful to Sister Rita Keegan of the Maryknoll Sisters, for all that she did for me in the immediate aftermath of the tragedy in Bolivia and for her contribution to this manuscript. I would like to thank the careful, loving critique of Sister GilChrist Lavigne, ocso of Tautra Abbey, Norway, and express my appreciation to my Benedictine superior, Sister Juliann Babcock, and my community in Beech Grove, especially Sister Mary Sue Freiberger and Sister Harriet Woehler, who journeyed with me those tough years after the accident. I am grateful to Peter O'Toole of Galway, Ireland. My thanks extend to my Funk family—Jim and Marina, Edward, Kevin and Laura, Evelyn and Sidney, and Carolyn. A special blessing is my sister-in-law, Marina Campero Funk, who irrevocably linked all of us Funks to Bolivia.

I apologize for any oversights, omissions, or errors I've committed. As in any experience, there is an inexhaustible palette of perceptions that color any series of events. I take full responsibility for the fact that this book is simply my own construction—based on my own memory and from what became known to me later. I'm sure that sharper insights will evolve over time. For now, however, this is the written form of the story as I remember it.

Introduction

In *Story of a Soul*, St. Thérèse of Lisieux shares an encounter she had with God:

> I don't want to enter into detail here. There are certain things that lose their perfume as soon as they are exposed to the air; they are deep spiritual thoughts which cannot be expressed in human language without losing their intimate and heavenly meaning; they are similar to ". . . the white stone I will give to him who conquers, with a name written on the stone which no one KNOWS except HIM who reveals it."[1]

As Thérèse knows, speaking of encountering God is precarious.

---

1 From: *Story of a Soul: The Autobiography of St. Thérèse of Lisieux* by John Clarke, OCD, 2nd Edition (Washington, D.C.: ICS Publications, 1976), p. 77. The capitalizations are in the original. The quotation refers to Revelation 2:17.

In writing this account of that meeting, I'm very aware that I risk at once aggrandizing myself and/or soliciting pity, both of which would be unfaithful to the radical experience of total dependence on God's deliverance that I underwent. This is why, for the last twenty-five years, I've tried to discern from God when and what God wants me to share, and with whom God wishes me to disclose the intimacy of those moments and with what words.

Even though I've narrated the events of the night of January 21, 1984, several times to a few receptive audiences over the years, I resisted writing the story down until now. It defied my abilities as a writer, and I found it too emotionally challenging. I prayed long and hard over whether the time was right to bring this account to a larger audience, and came to the conclusion that it was. I am older, more seasoned, and perhaps more skilled in knitting together the disparate emotions that have clustered around the many paradoxes contained in what I call "the event." I've also been able to frame the story within the larger context of my vocation, and that has helped me understand its continuing resonance for me and my relationship with God. I've come to see that this is no longer my story, but perhaps a tool from God with which to help others.

Into the Depths is divided into three parts. The first third narrates how I became a nun, some of the great challenges and blessings I found in taking my vows, and what precipitated my journey to Bolivia. The second third is given over to what happened that January night, and the days immediately following the accident. The final third of the book concerns the flood of emotions and negative thoughts that followed my return to the U.S. and that now proved deeply threatening to my equanimity and the spiritual life I had chosen. Eventually, I found a language for what I was undergoing in the saving graces of the sources of my own Benedictine monastic tradition. I see these three parts as a triptych of the trials and moments of grace that form part of the larger story of the meaning of vocation, and of the way God is discerned in our lives.

In writing this book, I've been particularly concerned not to offer easy conclusions, full of platitudes about faith and wholeness, about the various epiphanies that I mention. While I believe my faith has deepened and I've grown as a spiritual practitioner, I am still a novice. I'm neither perfect, at peace, nor healed of the tendencies that have caused me and others distress. Indeed, I hope this book illustrates that our failures and blind spots are as instructive as the *tremendum*—the awe-inspiring and terrible beauty—that has revealed itself to me on several occasions. Both light and darkness show God's love for our fallibility and our ceaseless dependency on our Creator.

It's also beyond the scope of this book to name all the paradoxes of faith, let alone attempt to try to resolve contradictions, like God's pattern of testing those our Lord most loves. I've come to believe that these apparent contradictions are a satisfying way to hold opposites together in the faith of God's mercy, recognizing that it would be untrue to my experiences to resolve tidily all that remains unknowable. Some things remain ineffable, excluded from our full understanding because, as St. Paul says, "we see in a mirror, dimly" (1 Corinthians 13:12).

Furthermore, efforts to resolve all questions neatly—as well as to assign blame or apportion guilt too easily—remove us from the heart of the mystery of our relationship with God. They allow us to turn away from our fear, vulnerability, and weakness. Suffice it to say that it's clear to me that I and others made terrible mistakes and errors of judgment that more than explain the suffering and loss that occurred that night, without recourse to theories about divine retribution for past sins or the supposed capriciousness of God. Indeed, my realization that speculation and analysis are futile has led me to what the mystics saw as an inner practice of "unknowing"—peeling away the layers of our supposed understandings of the divine until we are left with the radically simple proposition that I am and God is. It is in this space that I now choose to rest my heart.

Finally, it's vital that I acknowledge that, although this is my story, each of us has stories that need to be told and listened to. If I've learned anything in the course of my life, it's that we encounter God through our own personal experience, and that to ignore that experience is to ignore God. While God respects our autonomy, God wants to be up close and personal in this life as well as the next. As I've realized, however, this deep love and attention can be overwhelming. In the words of Hebrews 10:31, "it is a fearful thing to fall into the hands of the living God."

PART I

The Invitation

1

Beginnings

I was born on October 15, 1943, in Earl Park, at the northern edge of Benton County, Indiana, the third child and second daughter of Bernard and Mary Hannon Funk. My father, of third-generation German descent, was the oldest of eleven children born to Edward and Jennie Funk. Dad and his six brothers started an agricultural business that employed 150 people. At the beginning of the 1930s, Edward J. Funk & Sons produced hybrid corn for seed.

My father had farmed since he was a boy, but I only knew him as a businessman, dressed in a suit and tie and going to work in the town of Kentland. My father had a law degree, but his role as president of the company was to look after the finances and arrange loans through the Chicago banks ninety miles to the north. At his death in 1989, Edward J. Funk & Sons had 59,000 contracted acres of seed corn in production, although by that time the family company had been sold to British Petroleum.

My mother was born and raised in the city of Indianapolis. Her father grew up near Galway, Ireland, while her mother came from Killala Bay in County Mayo. Mom shared with her father a love for the written word and Irish history, and had a degree in social work from Indiana University. An aunt, Mary Finneran, who was an Irish immigrant who worked as a seamstress at the family household of Franklin Roosevelt in New York, paid for her studies.

After they were married in 1938, my parents moved to a 100-year-old house on a 160-acre research farm. Our farm was an experimental nursery to serve the needs of the seed-corn business located in town. Although for four or five summers I worked detasseling the seed corn on a crew with other local kids from northern Indiana, I wasn't very engaged with the life of the farm.

My parents were dedicated to knowledge and learning. My mother was valedictorian of her high-school class and read Latin with ease. When she was in her sixties and seventies, she'd watch the Purdue University channel on television and take long-distance learning courses in mathematics. She particularly enjoyed giving extended reviews in her book study group. My father would often stop off at the Kentland library on his way home from work to read the periodicals, while my mother subscribed to as many as thirty magazines—

such as *America, Catholic Digest, Time,* and *U.S. News and World Report*—that arrived through our mailbox each month. My parents worked hard to provide us with cultural experiences beyond our rural culture in northwestern Indiana. We frequented the museums in Chicago and attended the operas at Purdue University in West Lafayette.

My parents' temperaments couldn't have been more different. Dad, as tall and stately as his own father, felt deeply responsible as the oldest son for his siblings. However, he also relished the success of his business. He drove a pale blue Cadillac, drank in moderation, and liked to play poker, in games where the stakes could reach four to five thousand dollars. His company furnished him with a $25,000 expense account (a huge amount in those days), and owned a resort in the Upper Peninsula of Michigan on Lake Gogebic, where we as children usually spent a few weeks in the summer. My father was a member of the Knights of Columbus, the Indiana Historical Society, and the Rotary Club, among others.

Mother was short and round, and more introverted and serious-minded. Unlike my father, whose German heritage didn't stop him from enjoying life, my mother had all of the intensity and little of the playfulness often identified with the Irish. In many ways, she had it hard, coping with six children and with no preparation for farm life. Although she liked the solitude of the wide open spaces, she nonetheless missed the closeness of the first generation Irish family she left behind in Indianapolis. And, as she lamented, Funks were everywhere—I had thirty-eight first cousins who lived mostly in a radius of ten miles—and I remember her complaining about how she'd married a clan and not a man.

Nevertheless, both of my parents benefited from the family's economic prosperity. Staff looked after the house, and us. Although to us children our parents seemingly brokered a tense relationship as a married couple, Dad was a good provider and Mom was dedicated to the home. All six of us children attended the local Catholic primary school in Earl Park from ages five to thirteen. The school enrolled about a hundred children, with double grades in each room. Because of the size of the school, and the fact that my father came from such a large family, I was guaranteed a cousin or a sibling in all of my classes. The whole school went to the traditional daily requiem Mass every morning, which meant we fasted until we got back into the classroom, where we ate breakfast that usually consisted of a fried-egg sandwich and an apple.

We were taught well by Franciscan Sisters from Mishawaka, Indiana (this was before the era of lay teachers in Catholic schools). In spite of the limitations of the rural background of the thirteen students in my class, most went on for graduate and postgraduate degrees. When we reached age thirteen, the four oldest Funk children were sent to boarding schools. My sister Evelyn and I attended Our Lady of Grace Academy in Beech Grove, Indiana, founded by Sisters of St. Benedict of Ferdinand, Indiana. My two brothers were enrolled at St. Bede's Academy in La Salle-Peru, Illinois, where they were taught by the Benedictine monks.

I loved school. Music lessons with Sister Harriet constituted my favorite class. Like my father, I was a joiner: band camps at Purdue and Indiana universities, 4-H, and Girl Scouts. My first real job was lifeguard at the Fowler pool, to which I drove in my own car. I reveled in academics and, although I wasn't the top student, I was class president for all four years. The fall after my graduation from Our Lady of Grace Academy in 1961, I entered the novitiate of Our Lady of Grace Monastery with four other candidates.

-<-->-

People are often intensely curious about those who feel called to holy orders or the monastic life. However, entering a religious life was neither considered unusual nor strange when I was young. My sister Evelyn entered the convent in 1960, and, although she rarely talked about it, my mother joined the Sisters of Providence near West Terre Haute, Indiana, directly after high school. She stayed in the convent, where she was known as Sister Philip Neri, for four years.

From a very young age, I'd been attracted to all things

sacred, which made my religious vocation almost an automatic progression. As a child I was fascinated by my thoughts. I recall particularly one episode when I was about three years old. I was sitting on a radiator swinging my legs and looking at my family and asking myself the question: *What was real?* Was it what I saw in front of me—the grown-ups and children talking in the dining room and living room— or what was inside me—a sense of myself and an invitation and attraction to the inner world? I remember banging the heels of my little white shoes on the radiator in time to the question: *Which is real? Inside or outside?* Even then, while it was obvious that there *was* something real outside of me, it was also self-evident that, when I shut my eyes, something else was inside me—an interior reality that had as much presence and weight as the world outside. When I banged my heels on the radiator with my eyes closed I could be in both of those worlds. In this way, I was aware of the interior and exterior worlds that every young person knows, but which knowledge is obscured as one gets older.

I was a devout child and I enjoyed being a good girl. I had vivid memories of God being all around me when I lay on the lush green grass amid the grove of trees at the farm and looked up at the clouds. God was present for me in our family rosary that we said each night before bed and at Mass at St. John the Baptist Church in Earl Park. I loved to pick and place flowers before the statues of the Blessed Mother.

As I grew older, I more and more felt an explicit invitation to give my life to God.

Clearly, the family I grew up in was Catholic, and there was indeed a culture among German-Irish families such as my own for some members of the family to "go to the convent." The Benedictines at my boarding school made a deep impression on me, not least because they were in their first fervor of starting a new monastery. I, of course, shared their excitement, but I nevertheless enjoyed all of the social aspects of being a teenager. As a lifeguard at the local pool I had more than my share of offers to go to parties and gatherings from other teens my age, even though I went to boarding school during the academic year.

Our Lady of Grace Academy provided me with every option to go to college and pursue a professional life (at the time I had ideas of becoming a lawyer). Nevertheless, I was intensely aware that going to college would effectively be an invitation to follow the direction of marriage and life as wife and mother, and that now was my time to pursue the question I'd asked myself as a three-year-old. Even though I loved children and would have liked to have a family of my own, I knew that a husband, marriage, and home were not my calling. Indeed, I had a kind of urgency in wanting to be engaged in what I saw as the work of God: prayer, solitude, and the monastic life itself.

I felt total freedom in handing over my whole life in

obedience and faith to God—a freedom that allowed me a degree of emotional calm in the weeks prior to entering the monastery. During that time, I would consciously count off the moments: "That's the last time I'll take a swim as a lifeguard," or "That's the last time I'll drive a car!" I was convinced in my heart of hearts that if I wanted to give my life to God I needed to leave everything behind. I also was keenly aware that even good things had to be renounced for the sake of something better.

In the end, no one—either my family or my teachers—compelled me to become a nun. Actually, I had to make a case for it and follow my own inner clarity. I felt called by God, and if God wanted me to be a nun, so did I. If God was to be found at the convent, then that was where I would go. I didn't know what God wanted, but I was eager to give it my all in trying to find out. If God had given me the gift of life, then I would return it in God's way; and the sooner I did this the better. In that sense, entering the monastery was not so much a renunciation of myself as an acceptance of all that God was for me: an attempt to answer that question of *which is real?* to the greatest extent possible.

2

Vocation

Accompanied by five other young women, I entered Our Lady of Grace Monastery in Beech Grove as a postulant on September 8, 1961. I was seventeen years old. Although I'd been accepted to three colleges, I felt deeply that Our Lady of Grace was where I needed to be.

Even at such a young age and in my zeal to follow God, I understood that, like the Catholic Church itself, the convent was simply the form, and one form among many, in which I would place my hope to follow God wholeheartedly. I never thought that either the Church or the monastery *was* God, or that God would *only* be found in those establishments.

Nonetheless, in spite of my separating the very fallible institutions of the religious life from the abiding presence of God, my relationships with the Church, clergy, and the monastery have sometimes been fraught with difficulty. What sustained me throughout was that I never felt betrayed by God or that God was remote from me. God was a solid reference for me, even though I soon felt lost and confused because I lacked skills and training in discernment. God was there, but where was I?

No amount of faith and zeal could have prepared me for those first years. I was intensely homesick, which is not unusual for me. When I'd gone to summer camp at Fort Scott, Ohio, at nine years old I'd been so unhappy that I cried incessantly. Later in my life, every time God called me to be uprooted when obedience to my superior demanded me to change my assignment, I experienced the force of gravity pulling me back to appreciate the life I'd lived before. Each time I settled into what I thought was doing the will of God, I'd feel the pull of the next move toward God. I missed the farm's orderly routine amid the seasons; the city seemed loud and busy. I felt out of touch with myself and with the nature that sustained me in my youth.

We five novices were to spend our first four years in training before we went out on mission. We took twenty hours of classwork and forty hours of homework each week for our bachelor's degrees in education. Priests would come to the monastery to instruct us in the usual college courses, while the prioress would always teach a class on the vows. When we weren't studying, we were chanting in the choir or doing manual labor. I took it upon myself to read the entire Bible and memorize the psalms. We were all expected to recite by heart the founding document of our order, the *Rule of Benedict*, on our knees in front of the novice mistress seated behind her desk.

While I understood I'd entered a disciplined life, I hadn't expected the monastery to be as strict as it was. Especially in the days before the Second Vatican Council (or Vatican II) from 1963 to 1966, I was immersed in an environment that hadn't changed since the Middle Ages. The monastery was full of strange rules, one of which was particularly severe. My sister Evelyn, who'd entered only months before me, had finished her postulant year and was a novice. Novices were not allowed to talk to postulants, except after lunch at recreation periods (which consisted of volleyball no matter what the weather was outside), and on Sunday afternoons. The following year, when I was a novice, I found that we were as severely restricted in talking to the junior sisters. So, for my first two years in the convent I was in the same building as Evelyn, and had all the same prayers, meals, and sleeping quarters, but was barely able to converse with her. To leave family and home to become a nun was one thing; but I was shocked at the imposed separation of blood sisters in training to become religious sisters.

The *horarium* (schedule) was so rigid that most of the non-verbal language was choreographed into an absolute form: bowing, walking in rank, eating in the prescribed way, doing our duties, etc. We'd rise at 4:45 a.m. and pray in Latin until breakfast, which consisted most of the time of toast and coffee. We then had a period of cleaning and classes until lunch, followed by an hour of recreation. In the afternoon were more classes and prayers, followed by dinner and another period of recreation. Compline was the last service of the day, and was followed by nightly silence. Lights were out by 9:00 p.m. We slept in large dormitories with as many as twenty-four beds in a room that were separated by wooden partitions.

We dressed in the habit that had changed little since the tenth century, even down to the nightcap we wore in bed. We prayed when we put on our clothes and sanctified each hour of the day with another prayer. We prayed short prayers to collect indulgences, and we prayed in between times. We were allowed to talk (to some people) for one hour a day during the week, during recreation periods, and during the afternoon on Sunday. Permission had to be sought and granted for everything, including trivial matters such as moving a chair or acquiring toothpaste.

What was most challenging, however, was that while the entire rigor of the monastic life required a great deal of discipline, almost no attempt was made to explain its benefits. Naturally, many of us wanted to know why we were performing the various penances or undertaking certain labors, and no one among the older members of the community seemed to know the answer, except that this was the way things had been at the originating community in Ferdinand, Indiana, from whose 500 members all 113 nuns (including thirty musicians) had come to Beech Grove. This was the way they themselves had been taught to be nuns, and that was all that mattered.

I have come to understand that these monastic observances were hallowed means of remembering the vows you'd taken, and that they had to be undertaken willingly for the sake of having an inner relationship with God. However, at the time, no one taught the link to the ancient tradition of humility, and little awareness existed of either the origins or content of what may have been fifteen-hundred-year-old rituals or practices. Instead, the monastic culture of the early 1960s was short on spiritual insight and long on observance of the letter of the law. These customs and rules were effective means of establishing and maintaining the monastic subculture. I saw why my own mother had left the convent. The atmosphere itself was stifling and the requirement of obedience made no sense to her.

These conditions were not unique to Beech Grove. The medieval feudal system existed in most religious communities before Vatican II. Nor was the religious life in the early half of the 1960s universally oppressive, and some of my nun friends report happy formation years. However, I can identify with the many books that detail the culture of misguided penance and strange incidents of delayed emotional development that existed.

What was ultimately missing was the crucial inner work toward God. Amid all the talk of rules and regulations, the study of theology and scripture, and during the long hours in church, there was little chance to share the experience of deeper faith and apostolic zeal. As a result, the climate in the monastery veered between the extremes of stern law and order to casual and occasionally boundary-less relationships. The legalism and conformity heightened both neurotic guilt and punitive judgment of others. Some of the elders, although neither harsh nor mean, had been trained in the old ways, and seemed to be depressed and hypercritical. Others, who were younger, appeared to be as bewildered as those of us in the novitiate. Between some nuns who wanted to be our strict parents and others who wanted to be our siblings, several of us found it hard to know how to relate to our community on a day-to-day basis.

Institutional and individual hardness of heart broke down my spirit, and I suffered acutely. If it was necessary to be humiliated, I asked myself, then how would I find some kind of solid grounding beneath my brokenness? Did my spirit need to be crushed to purify my soul? Was pride the root cause of my dissatisfaction and therefore was it my fault to feel so much distress? I was not only profoundly confused but disturbed that the adults around me seemed unable to help us develop (perhaps their own parents had been no help to them either). I felt the confusion particularly surrounding my academic efforts. I was that same outstanding student who'd been blessed with gifts during high school. Yet those very same teachers who applauded my achievements were now grim and critical and doling out punishment for the same stuff I'd been praised for just months earlier. Was it wrong for me to be an achiever?

I considered myself one of a new generation of women who wanted to give the whole of their life to God, not simply to serve the Roman Catholic Church or become a member of an order of nuns. Fortunately for me, Vatican II eased out some of the inhibiting aspects of monastic life in favor of a theology of humanism and holiness that promoted health and service to others. The focus back to serving the people of God rather than the internal needs of the Church was welcome, too.

This isn't to say I didn't see the need for certain constraints. My sister Evelyn continued to find monastic life very restrictive. She disliked the intensity of the silence and the emphasis placed on academic study for the sake of being a school teacher, which was the only career path open to nuns at that time. After fourteen years of monastic life, she left and married. I felt her loss acutely; it was a shared vision abruptly divided.

I, on the other hand, enjoyed the solitude and academic study. I needed the boundaries and prayers, and felt very drawn to the high-minded ideals of seeking God. I loved the

Divine Office, chanting the psalms, and studying scripture. On reflection, even the years before the reforms of Vatican II proved beneficial to me as a catechist, since I knew the old and the new. I can honestly say that, in spite of its strictures, the pre-Vatican way of life never caused me to regret becoming a nun. Although I entered very young, I believe to this day that it was helpful for me to enter religious life before I engaged in relationships that would have led to marriage. My discernment wasn't whether I should have entered the convent or not, but where God was calling me so that I could be closer to my heart's desire.

≺≺--≻≻

After four years of training, I was sent on mission with Sisters Carlene, Marie, and Bernardine to found and then teach at St. Barnabas School, on the south side of Indianapolis. We moved our trunks with the enthusiasm of beginners and created a small Benedictine convent. We worked hard to make the school Catholic in more than name. With Father Sciarra as the pastor, St. Barnabas flourished and we needed additional classrooms after only the second year. It was my task to teach forty-four fourth graders (including four sets of twins). I was also able to continue expanding my knowledge. The superior at St. Barnabas was taking her comprehensives for a master's degree at the University of Notre Dame, and I read every book on her reading list. The list was long and the paths of knowledge steep and deep. But my mind soaked it up like a thirsty traveler drinks water.

Vatican II had provided such a disjuncture for both elder and junior nuns that orderly formation of younger members was nigh on impossible; we'd been presented with a set of new freedoms that were difficult to process. One such example of the change was that, in 1968, for the first time in six years, Evelyn and I were allowed to return to our parents' house near Kentland. When we arrived, the table was set with the finest china and silver. Goldie, our collie dog, had a bow tied around her neck, and a huge *Welcome* sign was posted in the yard.

If I'd been struck by the dissimilarity between my life at St. Barnabas and Our Lady of Grace, then the difference between our restricted existence in the monastery and the privileged family life was almost paralyzing. I felt caught between two worlds, like Abraham on his journey from Ur to Palestine. I'd found God in my comfortable family farm, and yet it was difficult to find God at the monastery. So, I had to ask myself: If the monastery was not about God, then, what was it about? I wasn't "at home" in the place where I'd grown up, and my new "home," the monastery, wasn't yet providing me a place to dwell with God. I was ready for sacrifice, but felt a burden of unnecessary suffering that prevented wholehearted service to others.

I found teaching enjoyable and stimulating. Teaching fourth grade in a brand new elementary school was clear and doable. (After all, only four years previously I'd been giving swimming lessons to nine year olds!) Nevertheless, since I was still in formation and not yet under my final vows, I was required to come home to the mother house for classes each summer. The contrast between the small scale of life in mission and the large formal mother house, which now had 150 members, couldn't have been starker.

Looking back on events of over forty years ago, it's clear to me that the trauma of my early years at the monastery not only led to psychosomatic problems with my eyes and ears, as well as bouts of the flu, but also was directly linked to a steady clinical depression that had by the summer of 1968 become acute. I still felt deeply committed to the monastic way of life, and nothing to me appeared as compelling as my original *yes* to follow both my inner and outer attraction toward God. And yet I felt that I'd gone wrong. I was worn out, as if the life I'd lived over the previous seven years had sapped every ounce of psychic strength from me, leaving me with no more reserves to make sense of what was happening to me.

Each day, I woke up and went to bed unhappy. Sometimes I cried, but at other times my sadness went beyond tears. Nothing gave me any pleasure, and because I could see that others were gaining enjoyment from the meals we ate, the films we watched, or the flowers we planted, I knew that I didn't enjoy even the good things in life. More distressing still, every waking moment was accompanied by a profound feeling of dread. I dreaded talking to people and dreaded the *thought* of talking to people; going out or staying in filled me with an equal amount of apprehension; every interpersonal relationship caused me nothing but dejection.

I knew I needed help, so I asked to be taken to St. Vincent's Psychiatric Hospital in St. Louis, Missouri. Because the Benedictines had a mission in the city, it was convenient to undergo residential treatment there rather than in Indianapolis. In those days, of course, a stigma was attached to mental illness in society at large, let alone to those who'd become nuns. St. Louis was far enough away from Indianapolis that no one would know what happened to Sister Mary Margaret.

I was at the hospital for seven and a half weeks. One afternoon I walked to the front of the hospital property and sat on some old cement steps. Every now and again, a train would pass by at a moderate speed over the railroad tracks a block away, its forlorn wail echoing my mood. It crossed my mind that were I to climb over the fence separating me from the railroad tracks, the train would be traveling fast enough to kill me right away should I step in front of it. However, I was so deep in my depression that I couldn't even follow through on the inclination to take my life—even as a fantasy. Indeed, the gesture seemed futile. As I looked at the trains passing by, I knew I didn't even have the ability to *conceive* of how death could relieve me of an existence that was my burden to bear. Killing myself wouldn't alleviate my condition because I was convinced that the same depressed being would accompany me beyond death.

I cried those dry tears that serve no relief. Neither the prescribed medications, psychoanalysis, or group therapy, nor any of the activities I was forced to take part in helped to ease my depression. I remember going to the little library in the hospital and checking out books by the Danish philosopher Søren Kierkegaard, the French writers Albert Camus and Jean-Paul Sartre, and even Shakespeare's *Hamlet* in an attempt to grapple with the dilemma of existence. But reading about the sickness is not the same as laboring under the burden of living in this particular human condition. I found myself precariously born.

It's almost impossible to convey in words what it felt like to confront the irreducible fact and *weight* of my being alive. It was as if my spine—like a rod that went from my head to my toes—had decalcified and no longer could prop me up. Nothing nourished me or provided me with the strength I needed to negotiate an ordinary day. Instead, I was filled with negative judgments that ate away at my mental and physical tissue, and stole away any pulse or vitality I had.

All I knew was that leaving the monastery and returning

to public life, marriage, children, and a career were not options. Nor at any moment did I doubt the presence of God. Yet, in some ways, this latter knowledge only provided its own kind of raw and naked pain: I didn't even have the choice to deny God's existence. I saw that while the confusion I'd suffered in my early months at Our Lady of Grace, the feelings of homesickness that had come over me and the sense I wasn't progressing spiritually, may have broken me down, my flirting with despair was a confrontation with my very existence as a human.

Ultimately, I was provided with a combination of drugs that enabled me to function at high enough a level to return to St. Barnabas. However, the drugs were too strong and interfered with my teaching. Moreover, keeping the convent schedule and teaching every day were still beyond my strength. So, during Holy Week and the Easter break in 1969, I asked to return to St. Vincent's.

On the night of Holy Saturday, a short service for patients was held. Holy Saturday is the darkest night in the Christian calendar—literally, it's the moment when the lights are extinguished as we keep vigil awaiting the resurrection of Our Lord in the morning with the rising of the sun. It's a reenactment of the day when Christ descended into hell, a state of utter hopelessness. We await in solidarity with the whole Church, as if in a collective tomb.

Amid the dim shadows of the shapeless, institutional

hospital chapel that evening I could make out only thirteen of us—all chronic, long-term patients too disturbed to be able to return to our homes. We followed the priest as he carried the Easter candle into the chapel, and I took a seat in a pew next to a bent-backed, toothless old woman. I felt my pride bitten—the pride of being a self-righteous nun: that I didn't belong with these other patients; that I should be wearing my habit and sitting in my rank with the other nuns at the monastery. Yet, as far as the other patients were concerned, I was just another inmate, as mentally ill as everyone else.

Well, here I am again, I thought.

As I stood in the pew and the candle was passed around so we could light our own tapers, a hand slipped into mine. It was the old woman's. We were not at the point in the service where we were supposed to give a sign of peace, so there was no need for her to make such a gesture. Perhaps she merely needed to steady herself and I was able to provide her with some balance. I'll never know. But the touch of her hand, a simple act of connection, shot grace into my soul. All of the personas I'd constructed for myself—as the daughter of a prominent family, as a bright student, and as a high-achieving monastic—were stripped away, and the realization warmed in me that merely being human together was as good a "place" to live my life as anywhere.

This recognition was, in some ways, the deepest form of my healing. My hubris was leveled by the liturgy of darkness in the innermost chambers of a psychiatric hospital during Holy Week. I was brought low—just like everyone else— and given life. I realized profoundly that, whatever confusing and harmful experiences I'd had over the previous eight years, nothing could touch this innermost heart, where I was always pure and loved and present to God. True, God felt raw and primal, but the connection was permanent, strong, and wholly available to me. It was a place of deep abiding and shelter; a well from which to draw strength, no matter how bad I might feel.

Even then, I knew I hadn't magically been lifted out of the depression. Later, I learned that this place in the heart is in everyone, even (or especially) the elderly, bent, toothless woman whose hand had found mine that Holy Saturday night.

3
Failure

A few days after Easter 1969, I finally returned to my teaching at St. Barnabas. Later that spring, the Archdiocese of Indianapolis hired me to be part of a team consisting of one priest, one lay person, and twelve nuns in the office of religious education. Of the nuns, four were Benedictines (like myself), four were Franciscans from Oldenburg near Cincinnati, and four were Sisters of Providence from St. Mary of the Woods, Indiana. The fourteen of us were responsible for teaching catechetics (the formal training of Christian doctrine as specified by the Catholic catechism), educating directors of religious education (DREs), and providing the curriculum with textbooks and media resources.

The job offered a huge contrast with my previous work. Archbishop George Biskup was eager to extend the vision of Vatican II throughout his diocese and understood that we needed mobility and further theological training to carry that out. Each of us was given a car, a credit card, and the option of pursuing a master's degree of our choice. I decided to enroll at Catholic University of America (CUA) in Washington, D.C.

In my classes, I was lucky enough to be surrounded by wonderful teachers: I was a teacher's assistant to Roger Balducelli, who taught the phenomenology of religion, and had completed his doctorate under the great German theologian Hans Küng. I took scripture from professors who were involved in new translations of the Catholic Bible. One time, I remember visiting Georgetown University to hear a lecture by French philosopher Paul Ricoeur on hermeneutics (the method of interpreting scripture).

I had classes in the sociology of religion, catechetics, liturgy, and ecclesiology. I appreciated the distinction that was made between religions (which are of human design) and revelation (which is God's mediation through human tools such as scripture and tradition). I listened to Professor Charles Curran mount and defend his challenge to the prohibition of birth control as specified in the recently released papal encyclical *Humanae Vitae*. Vatican II was studied as a current event, not like the previous councils of the Church—such as the Council of Trent in 1545 or the first Vatican Council of 1868. We read the original papers from Vatican II and followed the ongoing discussion. It was as if we were sitting with all the bishops and cardinals discussing these vital issues of our faith.

Those were turbulent years for the country and the Church. I was active in student affairs and attended a number of protests against the Vietnam War and the Nixon administration's policies in Southeast Asia. I lived at the Dominican House of Studies, and we put up many a protestor overnight—including the famous peace activist Daniel Berrigan—in our guest room.

I wanted to continue on at CUA for a Ph.D., but my community of Our Lady of Grace had no need of a doctor of philosophy, and so called me back to continue my work in the Archdiocese of Indianapolis. Nevertheless, over the next decade I went through the entire reading list for the Ph.D. and continued to study theology and catechetics myself in a systematic way, like a scholar. I would set up my monthly calendar and pencil in three days of seclusion for nothing but serious reading.

During those same years, I also earned another master's degree, this time at Indiana University's School of Adult Education. My degree was in group-process, with a particular interest in how groups came to decisions, a mode of study that had an immediate impact in, and relevance to, my life. During the 1970s, religious communities changed the way they arrived at decisions. They emphasized achieving consensus instead of procedures whereby one group outvoted another, the latter being considered a form of tyranny. I came to the conclusion, however, that all too often the elusive search for consensus turned into endless talking at meetings with no follow-up action or accountability.

-<-->-

The changes in society and the Church in the 1960s and 1970s, while perhaps necessary to shake up both institutions and allow more freedom and diversity in both, were far-reaching. By the time I returned from CUA in the mid-1970s, many of my confrères had left the convent and several of my priest friends had become laicized and later were married. From 1961 to 1970, Our Lady of Grace lost fifty sisters, and I was the only one of my entering class of five to remain in the convent. Indeed, those of us left behind felt somewhat bereft because of the enormous amount of work that still needed to be done. Our greatest difficulty lay in the inability to have a shared vision that unified the community. We were also so focused on our own human development that we became enmeshed in the self-help culture then becoming popular in society. Nonetheless, I returned invigorated by my time at Catholic University and attempted to meet the challenge of my work in the Archdiocese with my theological training and newfound skills in group process from Indiana University.

Over the course of the next decade, I was appointed director of a catechetical library resource center, and coordinator for parishes in the area around Seymour, Bloomington, and Madison, Indiana. Each of the twelve of us religious sisters assigned to the Archdiocese had a geographical area and an area of competency for which we were responsible. My teaching specialty was middle-grade students, the time of awakening to moral choices, which fit well with my interest in how one makes choices and sustains good resolve with right action that protects the weak and fosters creativity for the strong. As a team, we were responsible for a total of thirty-nine counties, which constituted almost half the state of Indiana and 220,000 Catholics overall. I visited twenty parishes each month.

One of my religious co-workers in the Archdiocese was Sister Gilchrist Conway, who was hired to coordinate adult education for the Department of Religious Education. Gilchrist had been born almost exactly a year before me on October 17, 1942, on Chicago's South Side. Her father was an accountant, and her mother, Julia, was a secretary in a large school. Julia was a superb organizer: each year she coordinated the Fourth of July fireworks in Chicago for a residential sanitarium for patients with tuberculosis.

I came to know Julia Conway well over the coming years. My parents' house near Earl Park was half-way between Indianapolis and Chicago on US highways 41 and

52, and I'd sometimes catch a ride from Gilchrist when she was returning to Chicago or we needed to head back to Indianapolis. Because our respective homes were both north of Indianapolis, Gilchrist would often see my family, and I hers, and this enabled us to be friends beyond just being co-workers at the office.

Gilchrist was blessed with a great sense of humor and a passion for life and activity. She stood about five feet six inches tall, and had a ruddy complexion, pale skin, and beautiful, lucid blue eyes. She played the piccolo and flute, and was an able singer. Zealous and creative, Gilchrist, perhaps typically for an Irish Catholic, had a considerable ability for rhetoric. Like most of her clan in Chicago, she was more Irish in identity than the Irish in Dublin.

Gilchrist had gone to college at St. Mary of the Woods, in West Terre Haute, Indiana, where my own mother was a nun for a few years. Gilchrist excelled in mathematics and journalism. She held a deep commitment to social justice, and worked several summers in New York at a shelter founded by Dorothy Day of the *Catholic Worker*. In 1968, she'd joined the Sisters of Providence, whose mother house was in St. Mary of the Woods. As part of her congregational vision, she'd dedicated herself to helping the poor and suffering in those schools and communities they served.

Gilchrist and I worked on the same staff for four years at the Archdiocese before she also became the executive secretary of the National Catholic Educational Association (NCEA) in Washington, D.C. in 1973, commuting from Indianapolis. At the same time, she enrolled at the Christian Theological Seminary in Indianapolis, and completed a doctorate of ministry in 1976. Her dissertation was an analysis of the differences in perspective between those Catholics who'd resisted the reforms of Vatican II and had changed in name only, and those who'd embraced the renewal completely in word and deed.

After her studies in Indianapolis came to an end, Gilchrist moved on to different assignments, although we kept in touch. I remained with the Department of Religious Education in Indianapolis, ultimately becoming the coordinator of the DREs, then director of the entire department. As a team we organized the curriculum and teacher training for the staff of the 160 parishes, seventy-six grade schools, and twelve high schools of the thirty-nine counties. We believed this work was not only our job, but part of our mission was to go from parish to parish talking about what the changes of Vatican II meant. We enjoyed engaging with people and training parents and teachers to be catechists.

We felt openness and eagerness among ourselves and in the people we met—a new commitment to social engagement and a renewed connection between the lay and the clergy through forming boards that implemented shared responsibility. When the eight or ten of us taught in the twelve deaneries for ten consecutive weeks, five to six hundred people would come to fulfill requirements for certificates in catechetics. It was an exciting time, and while some people opposed the changes taking place, most were very enthusiastic about belonging to a Church that was revitalizing itself, by allowing scripture to be more teachable and the textbooks more personal, and making itself relevant by returning to the sources of Christ Jesus as the center of our faith.

I thoroughly enjoyed my time in the Archdiocese. We worked long hours, and sometimes five evenings a week. I was still only in my thirties and had a great deal of energy. But I could see the Archdiocese was shifting. Many more lay people were joining our work, and it was evident they could do several of the jobs undertaken by the religious sisters. I once more turned my thoughts to pursuing the doctorate that had beckoned me ten years previously. I now had an opportunity to complete it: I was a published author on catechetical ministry; I'd conducted many workshops on the content of Catholic teachings; and I was on the board of the National Conference of Diocesan Directors where we initiated middle management systems for DREs.

As it stood, I had the potential to join the faculty for training priests at St. Meinrad School of Theology in Indiana, but as yet had no doctorate that would qualify me to have tenure. Since St. Meinrad was 150 miles from Beech Grove, the monastery where I'd professed my vow of stability, I'd also be obliged to commute from a third location or another convent that was not sponsored by my motherhouse.

Under such circumstances, I wondered how I'd be able to live as a monastic. The nuns I'd seen at CUA were living in little apartments away from their community, and it seemed to me that they'd sacrificed their vow of stability to a specific monastery in favor of living apart "on mission" as professors in the academy. I feared that I would not enjoy a similar arrangement. I also disagreed with some of the methods to train the priests, and was having some doubts about seminary education as a whole. Directives had come from the bishops that women weren't allowed to teach theology or be spiritual directors of students for priesthood. Religious and laywomen could only be staff in an academic department or teach the practical pastoral skills; however, they could teach nothing about the interior life of a priest.

Nonetheless, in 1982, in spite of all my reservations and giving in to the competitive part of my personality that loved learning, I received permission from my superior to return to CUA, to complete the requirements for a doctorate.

-<--->-

The difference I experienced from my study the first time at CUA couldn't have been greater. I was ten years older, and now had experience in teaching teachers and working on curriculums, as well as writing textbooks and evaluating what and how students learned. To my dismay, I found that, while the times had moved on, many of the professors hadn't. I found the teachers and classes stuck in the same content of a decade ago. Indeed, with the exception of Sister Mary Collins, OSB, professors and their teachings seemed worn out, dry, and without depth or passion. The priests seemed to lack fervor saying Mass; and, to my great distress, faith appeared to be absent at the heart of the theological education. Instead of being helped to understand the mystery of the resurrection, we were required to memorize the twenty-two discrepancies between the gospels of Matthew, Mark, and Luke (the Synoptic Gospels), and then cross-reference them. No matter where I looked—whether during the Mass or in the classroom, among the students or at meals in Caldwell Hall—I couldn't find a fraction of the animation that I'd assumed was fundamental to study in a Catholic university.

I'd loved my apostolic ministry and felt I was doing God's work. Throughout the 1970s, as I worked for the Archdiocese of Indianapolis, I'd had a presence of Christ Jesus abiding in my life. I felt on fire, like St. Paul, teaching the faith, which served to enhance my own zeal. To come to CUA, where learning had been seemingly stripped of all conviction and scripture was just another literature upon which to perform exegesis, was shocking and discouraging. My mystical life shriveled in the same place where ten years ago I'd thrived. All institutions have a life cycle and it seemed to me that CUA had sunk to a low ebb of vitality compared to just a few years prior.

I was soon confronted with the overturning of another assumption. To my growing discomfort, I sensed a disconnect between learning about faith, tradition, scripture, and the Church and my personal quest for an authentic spiritual life. I had naïvely or ignorantly believed that academic study would automatically lead to wisdom and mature decisions that would help me help others. The learning curve was steep, with requirements that I acquire more languages, read more books, and study up on this and that theory. Yet I felt that each theory and book I studied told me more about the writer and researcher than about God. Indeed, it seemed to me that the more I studied, the more my devotion toward God dried up and the less time I spent in prayer.

I was also turned off by the theology that posited that "God is dead," and which was popular in the 1970s and at Catholic U. This theology didn't strike me as just another theory but a personally dangerous pitfall into chaos and crisis. To me, it seemed that delinking reverence for God with speculation about the nature of God was reductive. Moreover, demythologizing and deconstructing every aspect of scripture and tradition offended my piety. As the time drew closer to my preliminary examinations, I became increasingly anxious about my academic future and the various deeply unwelcome decisions I'd be forced to confront.

One day, I stood before a window in my room that overlooked the Shrine of the Immaculate Conception and asked myself over and over whether I had it in me to be a scholar. Was God asking this of me? Was a life of study my calling? I remember posing myself the question, *Do I need to know more?* I only wanted to know God, rather than accumulate more information about God. Would a Ph.D. contribute to that knowledge? Or perhaps I didn't need to undertake three more years of study. I knew I already had a deep and powerful relationship with God, one that wouldn't be enhanced one iota by whether I parsed the twenty-two discrepancies across or within the Synoptic Gospels. My soul needed nurturing, not intellectual numbing.

As I stood by the window that day, staring at that mosaic design on the dome, I suddenly felt that place in my heart that had once been awakened by the old woman during the Easter Vigil service—a place inside me to which no more knowledge could be added or taken away. I wasn't critical of doctoral studies. I simply saw that I didn't need the "more" that such studies would require or provide. I realized with complete certainty that I actually already *knew* God, and that more courses might even take me away from my heart's desire.

Unfortunately, the moment passed and (as is so often

the case when I doubt my best instincts) I didn't pay heed to that insight, at least in my conscious mind. In an eerie parallel of the moment fifteen years before when I'd sat on the steps overlooking the railroad tracks, I saw no way out of my predicament. God, I thought, was offering me no clear direction, and so I took the preliminary comprehensive exams . . . and failed.

I took my failure very hard; indeed, so much so that in the summer of 1983 I voluntarily returned to St. Vincent's Hospital to benefit from more psychiatric treatment. Unlike in 1968, I didn't ask to be placed on any medication and this time I lived at a Benedictine monastery and commuted to the doctor as an outpatient from the other side of St. Louis. I was, however, full of self-doubt: Was I smart or wasn't I? And if I was the former, then why did I fail? If I wasn't to become a scholar, then what was I to be?

Looking back over a distance of almost thirty years, I feel confident that my inability to pass the exams wasn't because I wasn't intelligent enough, but rather that I was relying on my thinking mind to make choices that could only be made from the heart. In fact, my failure was a kind of defense mechanism to protect me from moving into greater conflict and distress later on. I cannot say for sure what I'd have done if I'd passed and gone on to write my dissertation, or how I would have dealt with the secular life living outside of community. I was, at heart, a monastic looking for the living

Word in my studies and not an academic. I knew I wouldn't be content to grade papers in an apartment somewhere near a university and struggle to be as objective as possible with new academic theories about God. By collapsing as they did, my body and spirit were ahead of my mind and recognized that my deepest hunger wasn't being fed. Consequently, my failure may have been my salvation. Or, to put it another way, God took charge of my journey.

Nonetheless, it was a very visible and public failure, especially for someone who came from a family that valued learning and education. I had, after all, read the entire list of books and articles required for the course. I had been published, and was considered a leader in the field I was studying. I was proficient in the course work and the theology was of great interest to me. When my own self-image was of someone who was always successful, such a disintegration—a second time, no less—was deeply humiliating. Why did I need a second round of being taken into the depths to be shown that I was nothing?

Once again, I felt Kierkegaard's "sickness unto death" about the future ahead of me. I'd already been contracted to teach at St. Meinrad's summer school, and had some writing commitments, both of which I finished with great labor and emotional difficulty. In order to get away, I joined some of my Sister of Providence friends on two ten-day canoe trips to Canada, and went backpacking and camping with a cousin and friends and family in Colorado, all in an attempt to get my strength back and figure out what I might be called to do.

I'd also reached what I felt were the limits of psychotherapy and counseling. By this time I'd undergone almost fifteen years of counseling, and it became harder simply to attribute my problems to my family of origin or my early formation in the monastery. That I had difficulty negotiating with, and adjusting to, developmental stages seemed a thin response to the way I felt. I certainly didn't regret the hours of therapy I'd undergone with skillful doctors, and it was interesting to learn about how human relationships, feelings, emotions, and motivations interacted with compulsions and other factors, such as the environment in which I lived.

But, for me, the greater value of these sessions lay in practicing humility rather than learning a doctor's diagnosis, which at times veered toward pop psychology. I found myself asking whether there was another way to follow God's directives and feel better from the inside that didn't rely on the diagnosis of specialists and one more consultation. Indeed, was it so important that the unconscious be fully manifested, and if it was, what should I do? Was self-knowledge all that one could aspire to?

I found comfort and healing in ordinary friendships. In the late 1970s, Sister Mary Sue Freiberger from Our Lady of Grace provided the steady support that Sister Gilchrist had offered outside the community. I also reconnected with my siblings, and we grew into the best of friends. Community life at Beech Grove continued to foster healthy friendships and ongoing dialogue as a skillful means to get along.

I also had found pleasure in my outside work. I was part of the first wave of sisters who had outside jobs rather than ministry in monastery-sponsored institutions. We were credentialed and competent professionals. Our elders led by example, and sometimes we overworked to demonstrate our zeal. Nonetheless, I was becoming more and more aware that missing from our work as teachers, nurses, and administrators was the training of the mind for service, of a sense of why we were doing what we did. We could, of course, point out that our jobs sustained the community economically; but again, this was not training in selfless apostolic zeal.

During the 1970s, Pope Paul VI had asked all Catholic monasteries to give ten percent of their community members to Latin America. Our Lady of Grace had staffed a mission in Cali, Colombia for over twenty years, with five to eight sisters living and working in very difficult circumstances. Perhaps, I thought, as I mulled over my options in the wake of my failure at Catholic University of America, I should dedicate myself to the poor, learn Spanish, and go to Latin America. I was far from convinced that I wanted to leave Indiana or even whether I had a call to be a missioner. Understandably, given my resumé and recent ambitions, I'd always seen myself as a teacher of teachers or an administrator, someone who enabled others to do the work of setting up shelters or food pantries for the homeless. At forty years old, I really wasn't sure what God wanted me to do with the second half of my life. I felt that my first segment was complete and I was weary from overwork and the rude failure of academic pursuits; but I was also up for my next assignment. I just needed to know what it was to be!

That fall I received an audiotape from Gilchrist, who was now more than two years into a mission in Bolivia. Gilchrist had visited India and had met Mother Teresa in Calcutta (now Kolkata), an event that had changed Gilchrist so radically that she decided she wanted to leave the Sisters of Providence and join the Missionary Sisters of Charity. I was with Gilchrist once at the NCEA Convention in Chicago where Mother Teresa was the keynote speaker and Gilchrist had a personal audience with her to discern her vocation. Unable to obtain the necessary visa to allow her to work and join a novitiate in Calcutta, Gilchrist realigned her goals and left Indianapolis in 1978 to become part of a team that serviced rural Catholic parishes in the south-east diocese of Tulsa, Oklahoma. I would drive out to visit her each year.

Ultimately, Gilchrist was able to enroll with the Maryknoll Associates, which was a new program established by the Maryknoll Sisters of Ossining, New York that allowed sisters of any community to become part of the Maryknoll pastoral teams for a number of years. Maryknoll

Sisters typically had more extensive training and tighter boundaries on what or who was accepted for missionary work than other orders, and to accept all these associates was considered a very liberal move. In 1980, Gilchrist was sent to the language school in Cochabamba, Bolivia, for two years to learn Spanish, before beginning the job assigned to her by the Maryknoll superiors.

In addition to Gilchrist's presence in Bolivia, I had another reason to be interested in the country. My brother Jim had married a Bolivian woman, Marina Campero, whom he'd met when he was a student at the Georgetown School of Foreign Service in Washington, D.C. Marina's father had been the head of the military, and Marina had shared with our family a great deal about her beautiful country. Jim offered to pay my way, and my superior gave me permission to visit Gilchrist.

Nonetheless, it was Gilchrist's own invitation that sealed my decision. She and I had kept in touch through letters and tapes, since we were unable to use the telephone. In an audiotape I received in the Fall of 1983, Gilchrist said words that were a balm for my soul: "If you ever need a place to come and just kind of be, or stretch out, or not have to get involved, or not have to fret, not have to do whatever it is that, oh, would distract you from being, come to Bolivia. We have lots of room; we have lots of beautiful fields and mountains. You're always welcome here. You can accompany

us in our work. But more than that, you can just be with
me."

The thought of doing just that—experiencing Gilchrist's
passion, sense of humor, and dedication, as well as getting a
break from the trials of the previous year in a completely new
place—was irresistible. Gilchrist's invitation would not only
allow me to fulfill that part of Pope Paul's request but enable
me to surround myself with new people and an old friend,
and provide me with an opportunity to discern whether I
was being called to missionary life in South America.

Because of other commitments, I was unable to go to
Bolivia until January 1984. I called Gilchrist's mother, Julia, on
New Year's Eve and told her I was going to go to Bolivia and
asked her whether Gilchrist wanted me to bring anything.
Shortly afterward, Julia called me up with a number of items
that might be considered useful but hardly essential to the
missionary life. The list consisted of a frozen turkey, two fifths
of bourbon, two boxes of five-pound Fannie May "turtles"
(which are pecans and caramel covered in chocolate), and
two bras!

I told Julia I'd bring this odd collection. These days, of
course, you'd never be able to get through customs with such
a motley arrangement, but we all had a degree of innocence
about airline security in the 1980s. I acquired a maroon vinyl
bowling bag that had the logo of St. Barnabas on it, to put in
a twenty-five-pound frozen Butterball turkey, the booze, the

chocolates, and two bras. In my own backpack I stuffed an extra pair of jeans, a skirt and blouse for church, hiking boots, a sweater, and a windbreaker. I flew out from Indianapolis to Chicago and then through Miami, Panama, arriving at Santa Cruz in Bolivia, and then on to the city of Cochabamba, Bolivia. It was January 11, 1984.

PART II

The Question

4

The Team

Bolivia is a landlocked country of great geographical variety. It has some of the largest peaks in the Andes mountains—as high as 21,000 feet—yet it also contains a substantial part of the Amazon rainforest in the east. At 13,500 feet above sea level, the capital La Paz is the highest major city in the world, seventy-eight more feet than Lhasa in Tibet. For those of us born and raised in the flat lands of the American Midwest, it's hard to appreciate the enormous scale of the Andes, which are, after the Himalayas, the second highest range in the world.

Bolivia's population is fifty-five percent indigenous— split roughly equally between Quechua and Aymara—with around thirty percent mestizo and fifteen percent white. Many of the Aymara, who also live in northern Chile and Peru, and the Quechuas, who are spread across Peru, Ecuador, and Bolivia, are very poor. Bolivia today has a growing population of Evangelical Christians, but at the time it was ninety-five percent Roman Catholic. The country was just emerging from a period in the early 1980s when a series of military governments marked by corruption, drug-smuggling, and human rights abuses, in addition to a collapse in the price of tin—one of the major industries in Bolivia—had debilitated the country's economy.

Cochabamba, where I landed, was then a city of half a million people. About 150 miles southeast of La Paz, it rests in a valley in the Andes range at about 9,000 feet above sea level, and after La Paz and Santa Cruz is the third largest city in Bolivia. January is the height of summer in the southern hemisphere and Cochabamba was full of flowers and grasses when I arrived. It was also the rainy season, and it rained every day I was there.

The team of missioners to which Gilchrist belonged consisted of four nuns and two priests. Rita Keegan had joined the Maryknoll Sisters after one year of teaching in 1957. She could speak Spanish and the native language of Quechua quite well. Rita was particularly concerned with community development and issues of economic sustainability. She initiated pastoral programs with the Quechuan Bolivians that immersed her directly in the lives of the ordinary people for over two decades. She worked closely with Father Matt Mueller, a Dominican priest from Chicago in his early sixties who'd lived in Bolivia for many years. Matt had been ordained in Rome and had a doctorate in theology from a university in Spain. He was deeply committed to aiding the poor and suffering.

Both Rita and Matt were very involved in working on homesteading projects near Santa Cruz. The Bolivian government would designate land in the rainforest for the indigenous Bolivian. Rita and Matt would write and obtain grants to fund individuals and groups to migrate and become self-organizing and self-sustaining communities. As a result of their work, both Rita and Matt had developed into extremely capable planners and logisticians.

Another member of the team, Mary Mahoney, was a Chicagoan and a Dominican nun from Sinsinawa, Wisconsin. Mary had a master's degree in fine arts. She was a simple and shy woman with beautiful, soft brown eyes, and a quick wit and generous laugh. In her forties, she had an introverted personality, was extremely sensitive, and I believe had a hunger for the contemplative life. Because her own community sponsored her, Mary lived with the other members of the team in Cochabamba on the weekends only, and was, as it were, "hired" by the team for their work.

The fourth nun in the team was Geraldine McGinn. Gerry was born in New York City on July 4th, 1937. Her early education took place in New York Catholic schools where she was greatly influenced by the Dominican Sisters of Sparkhill. She graduated from St. Helena's High School and entered the Dominican Sisters community, making her first vows on May 16th, 1956. From then until 1981, she was deeply and creatively involved in elementary and secondary education in the Catholic schools of the Archdiocese of New York, where she served as chairperson of the Community Council of her congregation for two terms and was very active in the various projects of the Inter-Community Center for Justice and Peace, organized by religious communities of the Archdiocese. In 1981, Gerry joined the Maryknoll Sisters Associate Program and in February 1982 became part of the mission in the Cochabamba valley.

Gerry's personality was the opposite of Mary's: she was gregarious and loved to sing, especially Broadway musical hits, and she even had a life-sized picture of Bette Midler on the door of her room. In another life, I'm sure she would have been a model and a dancer. Gerry and Gilchrist had met in the language school sponsored by the Maryknoll Fathers and, given their compatible temperaments, were, along with Rita, the best of friends.

The final member of the team was Jack Risley, a Dominican priest from Chicago. He was forty years of age and suffered from diabetes. Nevertheless, he was very eager to help in extending the mission.

◄◄–►►

Rita, Gerry, and Gilchrist met me at the Cochabamba airport in a borrowed jeep, as the team's 1952 sky-blue Willys jeep was in the shop getting new tires. Gilchrist presented me with a huge bunch of red roses. Although my backpack and I had made it from Indianapolis, the bowling bag with the turkey was not to come until the following day. When the airport finally called to tell us it had arrived, Gilchrist was hopping mad: "How come they didn't call us earlier?" she said. When we picked up the bird, the customs man informed us that it was illegal to have brought it in and that he should have confiscated it. He relented, however, and we brought the turkey back to Casa Rosario and refroze it. I remember that Gilchrist shifted from rage to false, demure gratitude when she realized that all that she had to do to get the turkey was provide the usual monetary bribe for the guard.

Casa Rosario was a mission house on the outskirts of Cochabamba that provided the home base for the students of the language school. Maryknollers used it for their regional headquarters, giving missioners a place to stay in the city. When the house was fully occupied, it slept twenty-four people—three or four beds to a room—with a bathroom down the hall. It was a very simple space: a dining room, a small chapel, a kitchen, a gathering place with windows on one side and bookcases on the other, and a fireplace.

Soon after I arrived, Gilchrist, Rita, and I visited the house of Doña Blanca, where we picked up a little boy called

Juanito Vargas, who was perhaps twelve or even fifteen years old, although he looked half that age. Juanito suffered from cerebral palsy. He was able to walk with a limp, but was knock-kneed and cross-eyed. He was also thought to be deaf, but nobody knew for sure as he was mute, and mentally and physically challenged.

Gilchrist had fallen in love with Juanito when she'd visited an orphanage in Cochabamba in 1980. She'd learned that Juanito had had a brother, but there was no record of what had happened to him. Obviously, the mother had been unable to take care of Juanito, so he'd ended up at the orphanage where Gilchrist had found him sitting on a bed wearing only a T-shirt. Gilchrist discovered that when Juanito soiled himself, the staff of the orphanage wouldn't change the bedding, but simply turned his mattress over and waited for him to soil it again. She knew she had to get him out.

At first, Gilchrist took Juanito from the orphanage on weekends, but one time she didn't return him and had to pay a fine. Finally, she decided to become his legal guardian, and began the officially authorized process that would allow her to do this. The Benedictines have a provision in their statutes that nuns cannot own anything, which, of course, extends to the indebting of the community with adoption commitments. Even though Gilchrist's order was more flexible in that it allowed individuals to acquire money for their ministry, I don't think anyone could have gotten permission to adopt a child!

So Gilchrist had a plan to ferry him to the U.S., where her brother Dennis and sister-in-law Debbie, who already had six children of their own, would look after him, while Gilchrist completed her assignment in Bolivia. Although the Bolivian government didn't place any obstacles to Juanito being adopted outside their country, the United States rejected the possibility because Juanito was mentally and physically handicapped, and an orphan. Therefore, Juanito stayed with Doña Blanca during the week and accompanied Gilchrist on her tasks on the weekends. At the time I arrived, however, Doña Blanca was due to have surgery and Juanito was out of school, so he was with us for the whole week.

Juanito was a delightful child, with huge, brown eyes and a ready smile and laugh. He loved cleaning dishes, sweeping the floor, pulling weeds, and hugging. During my stay in Bolivia I never heard the slightest negative word about him from anyone who was involved in his life, and everyone took turns looking after him. Every morning, when Juanito was with us and not with his family in town, Gilchrist would try to tickle him awake; and every night he would bless you and kiss you before you went to bed. In turn, Juanito thrived under Gilchrist's care. He'd put on about twenty pounds in the four years before I arrived in 1984, and although he remained very short (he only came up to my waist) he'd grown five inches in the same period and had undergone extensive dental work and surgery on his eyes to straighten them.

Gilchrist and the other nuns had also gotten Juanito into a school for the physically challenged, although this was also proving complicated. For diagnostic purposes, Juanito's school required reports from no fewer than nine doctors—some of whom gave contradictory advice on whether one or the other impediments would be attended to in this school. The Monday and Tuesday following my arrival, I accompanied Gilchrist and Juanito as we traveled around town to meet the doctors, only managing to see four of them. Further disappointment came when Gilchrist was given the official papers that indicated that Juanito had "failed" kindergarten at the school. The rejection had a familiar sting.

Taking on Juanito's care represented a serious commitment on Gilchrist's part. But she never shied away from selfless outreach, and Juanito gave her great joy. She had unlimited zeal, and although she was brilliant and could have competed with the highest-profile religious, clergy, or laity, she dedicated herself magnanimously to working for the least. Moreover, Juanito was always surprising them. Gilchrist and the nuns had taught Juanito how to signal his wants and feelings—thumbs up for "yes" or "good" and thumbs down for "no" or "bad"—and he was beginning to learn the rudiments of speech. It had become clear that part of Juanito's disability stemmed from the fact that no one had ever listened or spoken to him.

‹‹·››

Rita, Gilchrist, Gerry, Juanito, and I spent three days in Cochabamba, gathering materials for our trip to the *campo.* Rita drove the team's two-ton truck to the food warehouses, where we paid in cash for forty-pound sacks of flour, sugar, powdered milk, soap, and rice, as well as chickens for the food pantry and some bottled water and beer for ourselves.

We then traveled on to Charamoco, a little river village that lay southward about half-way between Cochabamba and Capinota, the capital of the province. About an hour (and one flat tire) outside of Cochabamba, we turned off the two-lane highway onto a gravel-and-mud road that snaked into the mountains. Now and again we came across creeks that we had to ford because there were no bridges. In spite of the mild temperatures, the altitude made it necessary to wear a sweater, except perhaps at noon when you might be able to wear a T-shirt.

Gilchrist and I sat in the back of the truck, coated in white flour that puffed from the sacks as our vehicle bounced along the rutted paths. Gilchrist's eyes shone: "This is the finest wheat we're giving them," she yelled above the noise of the truck's engine. I recognized the reference to Psalm

81, verse 16. "Even the richest in Cochabamba don't get this wheat," she beamed.

Finally, we arrived in Charamoco, which consisted of just a few houses. Rita and Carol (another Maryknoll nun) had a few years before engineered and overseen the building of a gray adobe house that overlooked the village and cornfields that were dominated by the Andes on all sides. Although the house had neither running water nor a pump, barrels trapped the rain that was funneled from the roof and this provided water for cleaning. Inside, the decoration was tasteful though Spartan. The theme was red: red wooden and cane furniture; red dishes, cups, and saucers; and curtains made of bamboo slats. The building sported perhaps the most comfortable outhouse I've ever known, with no odors and good ventilation. The house had been built on an old threshing floor, and the back rested on a spacious plateau.

That Wednesday I was designated to work at the co-op, where Juanito and I took the rice, flour, and wheat we'd brought from Cochabamba and poured each into two-kilo plastic bags to distribute to the people of the area. By noon we'd finished, and then as far as the eye could see *campesinos* descended from the mountains to fill up their *aguayos* (colorful cloths that they used to carry everything, including their children) with supplies.

On our arrival at Charamoco, we met the remainder of the team: Fathers Matt and Jack and Sister Mary. The two priests lived in a little house down in the village, while Gilchrist and I shared a small residence located about a hundred yards or so from the adobe on the plateau where four could sleep, two to a room. Each morning, Gilchrist would wake up and read her Jerusalem Bible. She'd memorized huge sections of her favorite book, Isaiah, and she loved to recite sections from Deutero-Isaiah. (The book of Isaiah is generally considered to have been the work of different hands. Chapters forty to fifty-five are associated with Deutero-Isaiah—*deutero* being Greek for "second.")

That Saturday night, Gilchrist and I had our own Communion service. I took some Eucharistic bread that Sister Frieda from Beech Grove had baked. Before I left Indiana, my Benedictine sisters had conducted a prayer service where they'd blessed the bread, and I'd brought it with me to use it for Holy Communion. Gilchrist, in turn, also blessed it. We listened to each other reading the scriptures for the day from the Lectionary and then we ate the bread. (In recounting the event this way, I show myself to be more traditional than Gilchrist. She would've said that we celebrated a real Eucharistic Mass, even though neither of us, of course, was— or could have been—ordained. I honestly believe she felt called to the priesthood.)

The next day, Sunday, Gilchrist had some time off, and we rose late and talked the whole day and into the evening. We took the opportunity to catch up over what seemed like a lifetime of news and conversation—although in fact we'd not seen each other for four years. We prayed and laughed together, and shared our hopes and aspirations. Gilchrist expressed to me in person the joy she'd communicated in her letters and tapes, and that, although the work was difficult at times, it was work she genuinely loved.

‹‹‹·››

January in Charamoco meant that the team was undertaking its planning for the next twelve months. The six members had a wide and complex set of responsibilities: they were required to perform baptisms, confirmations, and funerals, and visit every one of the four towns and thirty-three *pueblos* to say Mass and bless the sacraments, all in a cycle of two years. This was a considerable challenge. Some *pueblos* were only accessible by mule or horse, and a few only reachable on foot. When members of the team entered the peasants' houses, they'd occasionally find the occupants sitting on the floor, often with very little in the way of possessions around them. It was a scene, the team told me, straight out of the Palestine of Jesus' time.

Because of the great poverty of the region, the team had become responsible for pastoral care in its broadest sense. They'd set up youth organizations and a woman's group and were providing nursing services, while simultaneously trying to further their knowledge of the languages. In the short time I was in Bolivia, ten people a day or more would visit the house on the hill with problems they needed help fixing. One had a worm in his ear; another was a baby with a hernia. A man had stepped on a stick and it had sliced right through his foot. To each request, one of the team would open up their nurse's manual and try to deal with the situation, or if it was beyond their expertise they'd attempt to arrange professional medical help.

Sometimes what was required was beyond the reach of medicine. Gilchrist told me that once a woman had arrived at the house sporting a huge black eye. She'd told the team in Quechua that her sister had gotten mad at her and had hit her. One of the team patched up the eye and the woman returned home. About an hour later, another woman had turned up and was asked what was wrong. "I am sick at heart," she groaned, "I am sick at heart." It turned out that she was the one who had hit her sister in the eye and she was feeling remorseful. This confession entailed one of the team sitting outside the house with her for an hour, counseling and consoling her.

Gilchrist had given me some idea of the difficulties of the work—how so much of it was about tending to the maintenance needs of the team rather than the efficiency she knew in Indiana or Oklahoma where most of her time was given over to sharing the Good News of Jesus Christ.

The pace of life was slower than that in the U.S. she'd told me in a letter before I came—not least because everything depended on the condition of the roads and the team's jeep, and the weather. Among the native peoples of that part of the Andean plateau, she wrote, alcoholism and suicide rates were high as the people coped with problems endemic to poor, indigenous communities: disease, high rate of infant mortality, the uncertain crop yields of subsistence farming, and the challenges to their culture and lifestyle posed by modernity and urbanization. While Gilchrist recognized the difficulty of breaking through the people's natural resistance to change, she also acknowledged their extraordinary courage and resilience, the simplicity of their lifestyle, and their proven ability to make extraordinary sacrifices for their children and extended families.

Like many missioners, Gilchrist had discovered that although it was perhaps impossible to change the structures and systems that kept the native population marginalized, landless, and unable to move their societies forward, she and her fellow religious nonetheless had a vital role in bearing witness to the people's struggle and doing what they could to make their daily lives more dignified. In her typically honest fashion, she felt she succeeded on some occasions and failed on others. But she hoped she was growing in compassion, and expressed gratitude for being able to do such important work and to receive so much support from her friends in the U.S.

The planning that Gilchrist and the team were undertaking that Thursday was to last three days. As I heard the voices through the door to the room where they were meeting, it soon became obvious that the meeting wasn't proceeding very well. Juanito and I busied ourselves by sweeping the floor, tidying up the beds, going for a walk, and chopping and cleaning the vegetables. We made quite a team. I couldn't speak a word of Spanish, nor could he. He loved to take my watch off my wrist and put it on, over and over again.

Finally, later in the afternoon on Thursday, Gilchrist stormed out of the room. "Funk. We're stuck. You have a degree in planning," she said, referring to my master's degree from Indiana University. "Can you help us?"

"But I'm in grief," I spluttered. "You told me to come and hang out with you. I came to rest. I'm still trying to get over what happened at Catholic U."

Gilchrist gave me a look as if to say that she'd never heard such baloney in her life. "You get in there," she repeated, "and help us out, because we're in a real mess."

By this stage in my life, I'd been a facilitator for ten years. How could I say no?

So Juanito and I entered the room, and I got down to work.

What happened over the next three days was in some ways a privilege, as I heard presented to me in a very frank and honest way the concerns, assumptions, aspirations, and ideas for making a difference that these two priests and four nuns had for the year, both as a team and as individuals.

I offered the group the option of three types of mediation with myself as the facilitator. In the first, I'd be soft, as it were. I'd sit back and allow them to figure out what they needed to get done, and be present should they ask for advice. In the second path, I'd be moderately involved. I'd allow the conversation to flow and gently guide it by intervening when I had to. In the third, I'd give direction to a process and, once they agreed to it, I'd hold the six of them to it. Immediately, the entire team agreed that they needed to be directed as fully as possible because they were completely incapable of pursuing the meeting in any organized fashion.

I then took a ruled 8 ½ x 11 inch–sized pad of paper and filled up thirty pages by writing down all the team's assumptions: about who they were, who could or couldn't work together, what the problems were, what they were doing, and what needed to be done. In all, we arrived at perhaps two hundred assumptions (about how many parishes the priests could reach, who could or couldn't ride a horse, why women couldn't say Mass), and we wrote them down in outline.

In the assumptions, I got to hear all the problems, and they were all relational. It was the usual situation with teamwork, in that the functions and tasks were easy compared to the dynamics of interpersonal relationships. Gilchrist preferred to work with Gerry and Rita. Only Rita and Matt spoke

Quechua, which was the main language of most of the local people between Cochabamba and La Paz. Gilchrist didn't know Spanish very well, so she had to be accompanied by someone who did when she was involved with the native people. Mary was more of a contemplative: she needed a lot of time alone and wanted more of a transition period between tasks. Sometimes, the meeting arrived at an impasse: some members of the group were willing to undertake some tasks, others willing to do others, and the discussion was honest and raw. But we laid it all out so that the six could see not only what they were feeling and thinking but also know that each was being heard and heeded.

We then moved on with a question about mission: What was it that the team was attempting to achieve? Ultimately, they concluded that their mission revolved around a wish to bring Christ to the thirty-six destinations in their charge and treat every Bolivian as someone through whom Christ made himself present. From the elements that the team brought forward, we were able to string together a loose but workable mission statement. We then set two or three long-range goals that the team hoped to accomplish by the end of the year. Under those goals we established ten or so objectives, and then under the objectives we worked out who was going to do what task (whether in a team of two or three individuals, or solo), and how much time and how many resources it would take to accomplish that task.

Most people have about two thousand work hours in a year, beyond which they really don't have the energy or will to continue. Because of the logistical challenges posed by their situation, the team determined that the work-year consisted of 210 days for each member to dedicate to their mission. From this set amount of time, the team then decided which member or members would be able to visit the parishes, give missions, train catechists, build a church, or try to provide some social service in another place. They decided who would be the lead agent, and who would or wouldn't be part of the group for that particular task.

I recall that on that Thursday, I started with a prayer; on Friday, Gerry did the same, and on Saturday, Jack led while Gilchrist gave a homily on Isaiah 35—"The desert will rejoice."

"Isn't God wonderful?" Gerry enthused on the last day of the meeting. "God's not only going to make the lame walk, but to make them dance. God's not only going to make little Juanito talk, but to sing." Rita remembers Gilchrist's play on the words of God's allurement in the desert and how this attraction had gathered each and every person in the room to God's infinite manifestations. Because it was January, the theme of Epiphany after the Christmas season in the liturgical cycle was still present.

As this process unfolded, I realized the great strengths and dynamism, the passion and idealism, of this team—its honesty, its humanity, and its wish to try to work through the interpersonal differences toward accomplishing the goals they all desperately wished to see. I was in awe at their commitment. All the members had been struck by illness. Gerry had had hepatitis and Gilchrist had come down with the parasitical infection giardia so severely that they'd had to leave the houses where they lived with the villagers and move into the staff house. Yet their conviction and dedication to the people around them had only deepened over time.

The dynamics at Charamoco were so complex that it was a challenge to even design a plan, let alone execute one. The team all took risks in getting to some hard places to accomplish what they did. Mary, for instance, took on some major responsibilities, even though she was more contemplative and needed a lot of time to prepare and follow up. In spite of these six individuals' very different personalities, the desire for cooperation trumped lack of trust and fear of incompetence, and the team engaged in some of the hardest and deepest dialogue I've ever heard.

It had been two-and-a-half days of grueling work, but by four o'clock on the afternoon on Saturday, January 21st, we'd finished. We celebrated the accomplishment by singing a rousing *Amen* as Rita cooked the evening meal. The team had seven goals, forty-four objectives, and 1,200 days to give to the Lord. They were going to speak more Quechua and learn more Spanish. They'd attend the fiestas and live with the people. They'd make their team a priority, and they'd pray.

Recalling that session from twenty-five years later, I recognize that many might now see the limitations of planning and business models that don't necessarily apply to the conditions human beings experience in real life. But in those days, all of us were into planning and learning to collaborate as a team; and at the time, there was a genuine feeling that a new start was being made, with life-giving boundaries, clear roles, and felt expectations.

It wasn't all hard labor. On the evenings following the Thursday and Friday sessions, we gathered as we'd done earlier in the week for dinner. One of us cooked, while everyone else drank Manhattans. We played a short set of bridge and then ate dinner. In such congenial surroundings, I began to think the life of a missioner wasn't too bad!

◄◄·►►

After the meeting ended that Saturday, the team was to divide. The next day, the archbishop was arriving in Cochabamba to commission the catechists for their work in the Capinota region. The catechists were all lay Bolivian missioners and native people who spoke Quechua, for whom becoming a catechist was a significant and serious obligation. They were pledging to live in a village and to act in lieu of an ordained priest—providing the religious instruction and disseminating the teachings of the Church in the absence of any other religious authority. This commitment would require them to spend months, even years, away from their homes.

Mary, Gilchrist, and Gerry had spent months training the catechists, and the service would be at once the confirmation and highlight of a very important aspect of the team's mission. They were understandably very eager to see the catechists receive the honor and to wish them well in their mission, and so the three wanted to attend. At first, the plan was for Rita and Mary to go to the commissioning ceremony. However, everyone agreed that Mary had more of her Dominican-trained candidates in the ritual, so Mary, Gilchrist, Gerry, and Father Jack were designated to make the two-hour journey back to Cochabamba. Rita and Father Matt would stay at Charamoco for the Mass on Saturday evening and then drive to Capinota the next day to conduct Mass there.

That evening we ate dinner quickly, and there were no cocktails or games of cards.

Gilchrist turned to me. "You're coming, aren't you?" she asked.

I demurred, just as I had when Gilchrist asked me to moderate the team's meeting. I really didn't feel like climbing into a jeep for a two-hour bumpy journey at night, especially since I'd only arrived in Bolivia eleven days before and had already traveled the route less than a week previously. I also had an ulterior motive: the beauty of Charamoco. The house was simple, situated in a gorgeous location.

"You know," I muttered. "I just got here. Why don't I stay? I'll be fine. Rita and Matt are here, so I can stay with them."

"Oh no," said Gilchrist, in her insistent fashion. "No guts, no glory, Funk. Now you come along with us."

And so I did.

5

The Storm

I walked down to the little house that I shared with Gilchrist, retrieved my backpack, and packed my clothes for the next day. I was wearing my parka, my white shirt with its Oxford collar, a pair of blue jeans, a hat that one would go fishing in, a blue sweater, and my boots that I'd bought to go camping in the Rocky Mountains in order to clear my head after the examinations. I also wore a pair of hiking boots and carried a flashlight, in case of an emergency.

By the time we were ready to depart, it was nearly half past six. A chill filled the thin evening air and it was growing dark. Although it was summer in the southern hemisphere, the sun often fell behind the mountains quite early in the evening and rose later in the morning than in Indiana, where I was used to those lingering summer evenings and bright dawns on the farm.

We piled into the Willys, which although it was over

thirty years old, Rita had lovingly maintained. And now it had new tires. Father Jack was in the driver's seat and because I was smaller than the other nuns I sat in the makeshift middle seat in front, with Gilchrist to my right, by the door. Mary and Gerry were in the back, with Juanito on Gerry's lap. Stashed in the back were our little overnight bags, and some empty bottles and a few packages to take to Cochabamba. In spite of the achievements of the day, a cloud of disquiet hung over us and the air was uncannily still.

Even though Cochabamba was only twenty or thirty miles away, the journey would take us through the mountains and over difficult terrain, including across eight ditches, or *acequias*, before we arrived at the main road. Meanwhile, thunder and lightning over the mountains were providing a dramatic sound and light show; however, there was no way of telling from which direction the storm was coming, or where it was heading. It was also starting to rain.

As we religious always do before every journey, we prayed the *Memorare* together:

> Remember, O most gracious Virgin Mary, that never was it known that anyone who fled to thy protection, implored thy help, or sought thy intercession was left unaided. Inspired by this confidence, we fly unto thee, O Virgin of virgins, our mother; to thee do we come,

before thee we stand, sinful and sorrowful. O
Mother of the Word Incarnate, despise not our
petitions, but in thy mercy hear and answer us.
Amen.

Concerned about the increasing strength of the rain, I asked
Gilchrist if we ought to be making such a journey at such a
time of the day. She told me not to worry. "Let's just go down
to the river," she said calmly, "and we'll turn back if we can't
cross it." So, we slowly drove down the hill into and through
the village. Occasionally, thorny tumbleweeds blew across in
front of the jeep, the brambles sharp and strong enough to
puncture a vehicle's tires.

The rain began to come down harder and faster. Water
fell from the lush, green leaves of the tall trees that leaned
precariously from the top of the ten feet tall mud banks, and
swept over the beaten soil and pebbles that constituted the
road through the mountains. Then it cascaded in a steady
flow over the banks of eroded mud and scree that formed the
crumbling edge of the other side of the road, dropping into
the darkening valley below.

We knew there were only two *acequias* we'd have to cross
before we got to the main river. We managed to negotiate
the first crossing at the bottom of the hill just before we got
to the village of Charamoco itself, although we accomplished
this with enough difficulty to make me more worried.

"Do we need to do this?" I asked the group, as the jeep pushed its way through the water. "Don't you think we should stop and go back?"

"Oh no," came the nervous replies. "We do this all the time."

Outside of Charamoco we veered off the road into the bank. The jeep became bogged down and the engine cut out. Jack used his long legs to clamber out. He looked down at the tires, and managed to open the Willys's hood by unlatching the hooks from each side. He dried off the spark plugs so the ignition could catch and managed to get the engine running again. He then backed the jeep up, threw the gears into forward, and revved the engine so we could move on.

I remember an uneasy chit-chat in the Willys. It was clear to everyone that the roads were becoming more dangerous, although as we crept our way through the rain there was no consensus among us even to consider going back. At the base of my stomach I felt a familiar feeling of dread, the kind that wouldn't go away. As Jack gunned the engine and our collective prayer and the old jeep's efforts unclogged the wheels and we began to move, the fear stayed with me. Juanito also sensed the tension. Usually, he loved to ride in the jeep, but this evening he was fussy. Although I offered him the small flashlight I had with me to play with, he wouldn't take it.

"Are you *sure* this is worth it?" I asked.

"Oh! You're such a *gringo*," they laughed. And it was true. What did I know? I was from Indianapolis, and these women were from Chicago and the Bronx. Moreover, they had lived in this area many months, if not years, longer than I had. Jack himself had lived in Bolivia six years. Yet I wasn't confident. The night was now as black as pitch.

"Who's going to do the goals and objectives?" I asked, attempting unsuccessfully to match their strained lightheartedness.

Gilchrist turned and looked at me, and smiled. Then she said something that in retrospect was very strange: "Oh, Rita would be scared as well."

At this point the automatic windshield wipers failed, and because I was sitting next to the driver, I was obliged to move the little lever manually so we could see out through the rain-lashed windshield.

We arrived at a third gully, one either new or ordinarily so small that in normal circumstances it wouldn't even have counted as an *acequia*. At first, it seemed shallow as we drove into it, but it soon became apparent that it was much deeper than we'd imagined. The jeep immediately veered to the right and stalled again. Jack opened the driver's door and with his long legs he was able to leap from the vehicle to the dry land. I assumed he had gotten out of the jeep to size up the situation, but instead he disappeared into the night.

There was no time for reflection. The door on the driver's side was still open and I noticed water seeping into the bottom of the jeep. I leaned over toward Gilchrist and rolled down her window to show her the level of the *acequia*.

"Look, this water is really coming up through the floor," I said, rolling up the window again. "It's up to our knees. We need to evacuate. Come on, let's get out of here." Gilchrist didn't move.

Because I'd grown up on a farm and knew how to drive a four-wheel jeep, I climbed into the driver's seat.

"I can start this thing," I announced, seeing the old starter on the floor that one could press with one's foot. However, when I moved the wheel, I realized that the Willys's tires were no longer moored to the ground.

"This is going nowhere," I said, turning to Gilchrist. I knew Gilchrist was not a swimmer—in fact, I knew she didn't like to be in water—and so I pecked her on the cheek to make her react to a situation that was clearly becoming more dangerous by the second. But her face looked as though it was made of stone. She was paralyzed with fear.

I realized I had to get out of the jeep, but saw that I wouldn't be able to leap from the Willys to the bank, where there was dry land. It was just too far and, unlike Jack's, my legs weren't long enough. I could, however, get out of the jeep itself by swinging myself around the doorframe onto the hood, and then onto the top of the Willys, where I'd be in a much better position to be able to help the others climb out or, at least, enable them to hoist Juanito out of the vehicle and onto the shore.

I stood on the jamb of the open door, lifted one leg onto the hood, and swung my body over. I then climbed onto the hard roof of the jeep, where the rail that went round the perimeter would prevent me from falling off. I still held in my hand the flashlight that I'd brought with me and had offered to Juanito. I'd bought it in a double pack at a grocery store in Indianapolis as an afterthought. The pack included the flashlight and a little penlight. Ironically, I wouldn't have gone shopping if I hadn't had to buy the items that Julia told me Gilchrist wanted.

By this time I could see the lights of the jeep were becoming submerged in the water. I lay down on the hood, pointed the flashlight into the open door of the jeep, and reached in with my hand. I could hear Gilchrist and Gerry arguing, but with the otherworldly, slow-motion calm that sometimes happens when one is exposed to extremely stressful circumstances.

"I'll take Juanito," said Gerry.

"No, I'll take Juanito," replied Gilchrist.

"No, *I'll* take Juanito," I yelled. At that moment, I thought the child would be much safer on the roof of the jeep—as would we all, since the Willys was already filling up with water, and no one was evacuating. By now the rain and rushing water were making it almost impossible for us to hear each other.

I'd been on the roof for what seemed like two to three minutes (but may have been much less) arguing back and forth, when, to my horror, I felt the Willys begin to rock severely beneath me. This meant only one thing. All of us had failed to appreciate just how dangerous our position was when I'd taken the steering wheel and had discovered that the vehicle was no longer touching the ground.

I stood up to my full height on the roof of the jeep and realized that, sure enough, the jeep had turned into a boat, and we were beginning to sail, faster and faster, down the ditch that was meant to drain off water, but which had turned into a torrent with a life of its own.

I needed to take swift action. The jeep was now shaking and rocking violently, and I was having trouble holding my balance. I thought of Gerry, Gilchrist, Mary, and Juanito inside the Willys. I now considered myself to be in far greater danger on the top of the vehicle than those inside. If the Willys turned over, which was a very real possibility, I could be rolled underneath it and crushed to death.

I had to make a decision. I knew I couldn't reach the left side of the bank because it was too far away. However, if I jumped to the right, from my height on top of the jeep, the watercourse might be narrow enough for me to reach drier land.

I stepped back as far as I could on the roof, and leapt. I missed.

≺≺∸≻≻

Although it had been raining for perhaps an hour, it didn't seem possible that I wouldn't be able to hit the *acequia's* bottom, especially since even during the rainy season the ditches were usually passable and I'd jumped from perhaps five feet above the ground. However, my body met only water, and I was forced to kick back up to reach air. When I found the surface, I saw that the current was rushing me toward my left-hand side. It was still a narrow waterway at that place, and the stream boiled and rolled. I felt the massive presence of the jeep behind me and sensed its lights on my back.

Billows of thick, muddy water pummeled and pulled me beneath the surface, drawing me back up before again forcing me down. The depth of the channel through which the water was passing became deeper and the current more powerful than anything that I might think I had control over. I heard the harmonics change from crashing waves to an eerie quiet. Clearly, the jeep and I had passed under some kind of barrier.

I knew I had to get out of that waterway, because it was just rushing too fast and I'd either be killed by the jeep or slammed into the rocks and the wall of water spilling from the mountains. As I came to the surface again, in the half-light I caught sight of a branch rushing toward me. *If I get hold of it*, I thought, *I might be able to lift myself out of the river.* I prepared myself as best I could to grab it, and as I did I felt it almost pull my arm off. *We're going too fast*, I said to myself. *There's no way I'll be able to get out this way.*

And this wasn't the only danger. Because of the speed of the current, the waters had become like rapids, and I found myself hurtling directly toward a tree without any ability to swim against the current and avoid it. I drew my knees to my chest, pointed my feet in front of me, and braced for the impact. I hit the tree full on. A branch knocked my head back and cut a slice of skin from my right eyebrow down across my right eye and onto the bridge of my nose. I must have been knocked unconscious for a few seconds, because when I came to, I saw stars from the concussion. I lifted my hand to my face and felt it was sticky from blood. I recall thinking that one or two more of those clashes, and a tree wouldn't just slice my face open, but would cut me in half.

We were swept under another barrier. Suddenly, there were no lights behind me and the sound made by the water changed again. I was literally and metaphorically out of my depth and no longer in any contact with the jeep or, it appeared, the road. When I managed to come up for air, I found that, as I'd suspected, the water had taken me many hundreds of yards away from the road. The landscape had opened up, and I was being swept through fields in a valley scattered with trees.

The undercurrent was still strong, however, and I kept finding myself being pulled down deep into the water, where the current's strength surged this way and that. Pampas grass wrapped me up and turned me over as if I was a bale of hay. I knew from my time as a lifeguard that I shouldn't struggle to release myself. I had to remain as calm, relaxed, and alert as possible. If I tried to fight either the current or the bonds of the grass, I'd only exhaust myself or perhaps bind myself even more tightly in the pampas's strong grip.

I don't remember how long I was in the pampas grass, but before I had a chance to recover my bearings, a huge wall of water descended on me and I found myself falling what felt like eighty feet. The force of the cataract pummeled me and turned me over, until I finally hit the bottom of what revealed itself to be a major river—the Rio Roche. I was able to come back up for air and rest for a moment on a pile of debris to scan the situation. The river had broken its banks and had panned out like a lake, which while relatively shallow had spread wide for perhaps one or two miles from bank to bank. All around me, mountains extended upward about two thousand feet or more.

I started to feel the cold that until then I hadn't noticed. My teeth were chattering and began to ache. *I'm going to need a dentist when I get out of here*, I thought to myself, absurdly.

And then I distinctly remember adding, *You know, your teeth are the least of your problems!*

◄◄--►►

It's perhaps beyond my ability to describe what happened next, but before I knew what hit me, I was pulled down by several waves of water thudding into my back. I found myself in a very still place, with no motion whatsoever. My eyes were wide open, and my mind was completely present, intensely aware of its surroundings and what was happening to me. I felt totally calm, and a soft and diffused white light rested on my eyes, more beautiful and serene than anything I'd ever seen or been through before.

At that moment, a question came, as loving and gentle as the light itself. *Now?* it asked. *Do you want to come now?* It emerged neither from an audible nor an inner voice; I heard it only with what I would call my spiritual senses. It didn't present itself as some kind of reckoning. Instead, it was a confident and loving invitation to return. I had no doubt then, as I have no doubt now, about its source. I was known by God.

The question was posed in total freedom. In other words, I understood with absolute conviction that I could have agreed to die or not, but that neither choice was better than the other, neither was "correct" or "wrong." It was wholly my determination. In this silence, peace, and tenderness, God was asking me what I wanted and making it as evident as possible that the choice was mine, and mine alone, and that whatever I decided was full of grace.

My consciousness couldn't have been more alert; my critical faculties couldn't have been more awakened. My life did not flash before my eyes, as I've heard sometimes happens to those who undergo what are called "near-death experiences." This was no hallucination or other form of mental phantasm of a distraught mind: that was clear to me. I was emptied of the need to resolve things I'd done earlier in my life, or hold on to the ambitions I'd yet to fulfill. I felt neither remorse nor guilt, neither shame nor dread, nor any form of judgment. Instead, what came to the fore were the relationships that I held and valued—the being one with others in order to be close to God. I felt wholly present to God, in a full and unmediated connection.

It was the freest decision I've ever made, or am ever likely to make. I thought about my mother. She was seventy-six years old, suffered from a heart condition, and had a fierce Irish temper. I didn't want my life to end so far from home in a manner that would cause needless complications for my family and community. I had unfinished feelings about Catholic U., and hoped I might turn down this invitation until I'd made my peace with whatever and whomever had been part of my existence. I wasn't ready.

No, I replied softly and confidently in my mind. *Not now.*

Then I kicked upward and rose higher and higher in the water until I found myself on the surface, gasping for air.

I was alive.

◄◄--►►

The peace of that soft light in the face of death was completely opposite to the storm that surrounded me when I broke the surface. I spat out the water that had accumulated in my lungs from being so long under the river. The current surged around me and the thunder continued to roar above my head. Dead cows and huge trees slid by in the clayish, tan-colored mud that had been swept down with the rain and had merged with the river. I could make out mudflats dotting the vast expanse of water.

My training in swimming had taught me that, even though I was much closer to the right bank than to the left, I'd need to go with the strong current rather than exhaust myself, potentially fatally, by struggling against it to reach the nearer shore. I could see the swirls within the expanse of water, and knew that whatever strength I still had would be no match for the undertow. So I veered to my left, angling toward the mudflats, and let the current take me. If I could just get out of the river, I'd be able to pause long enough to catch my breath.

To my astonishment, I was still holding the trusty

Garrett flashlight in my hand. I skidded my way through the shallower water and managed to clamber onto one of the reliefs. I decided it would be easier to be rescued if I made my way upstream nearer to where I'd entered the river. However, as I walked up the mudflats, I found that the floodwaters were continuing to rise and there was no way I could reach the mainland. So I dropped myself into the current again, and sidled my way to another flat. Again, I walked in the direction of where I thought rescue might be most likely; once more, I found the way impassable, and seeing no alternative than risking the currents of the flood's undertow, I dropped myself back into the river.

When I reached the fourth island, I lifted myself to my feet only to discover that the ground beneath me was giving way. I recall distinctly telling myself very firmly, *No.* I wasn't going to be suffocated in quicksand. If I was going to drown, then so be it. So, I threw myself back into the water, and once more tried to direct myself to another island. Finally, I was able to pull myself up onto a flat that appeared a little sturdier. By this time, I was so exhausted I couldn't even stand up. I looked at my watch, which was still working. It read 8:40 p.m. I was to remain on this relief for another three hours.

I tried to lie down to rest, but I couldn't because I was short of breath and my heart was beating too hard, as hard as the thunder around me. I took my clothes off because they were wet and heavy with mud, and saw that my legs and thighs had cuts the size of those made by a dinner knife on them, the result of the serrated edges of the pampas grass. I was freezing, my body shaking and my teeth chattering, so I put my clothes back on. The night was colder than the chilled waters of the river, and I needed some shelter from the wind beating against my back and the rain, which was still pouring from the sky. Inadequate though they may be, my jacket and jeans were my only protection.

I also needed my clothes because, to my horror and indignation, insects began to crawl all over me, while others— ones that seemed long and armed with pincers the size of my hand—flew into my face. They gnawed any exposed area of my flesh, crept underneath my pant-legs, and bit at my hands and arms. Not only was this extremely painful, but it was infuriating. It's *insulting* and disrespectful to have your face eaten and your various orifices attacked in this way!

I grasped some of the thick, glutinous mud I was sitting on and began to slather it on any part of my body that was open to the air. What I didn't fully appreciate at the time, however, was that these creatures were doing me a favor. It wasn't just they who were drawn to the scent of death emanating from me: above me, through the flashes of lightning that illuminated the thunderclouds rolling down over the mountains, I could see three birds—buzzards— circling. I realized they were making plans for dinner, and I was to be the main course. I redoubled my efforts to grab as much mud as I could and covered my head, legs, and torso. Doing so not only kept me warm, but reduced the smell of blood that was emanating from me.

Applying and reapplying mud to my body, however, only lasted so long as a distraction from my immediate surroundings. Three hours is an age to be exposed to the cold, and it seems even longer when you're unable to do much more than sit on freezing, damp mud with your legs straight out in front of you. In the nearly two hours since I'd jumped from the jeep into the river, I'd been exposed to the frigid rain of a major storm. I'd been almost drowned in the flood and crashed against a tree, where I'd been cut across the face, and I'd been almost eaten alive by winged creatures.

Lying on the sandbar, I realized just how precarious my situation was. Pain surged from my lungs and abdomen. *I'll never live to see the light of day because this river is so much bigger than I am*, I thought. My head was bleeding profusely over the left eye, which was now wholly swollen shut as a result of my collision with the tree. One more blow, I knew, and I'd fall unconscious.

As it was, I was hyperventilating from trying to breathe the thin air at an altitude higher than anything I'd experienced in Colorado. Every part of my body that I could still feel seemed to have cuts in it, as though I'd been bound with barbed wire. And periodically I found myself doubled over in agony and retching from the decompression of the lungs caused by the altitude and "the bends." Each thunderclap made me shake with fright and the rain seemed like nails falling on my head.

It was as if the shock absorbers of the body finally gave out. Whereas before my heightened acuity had enabled me to make crucial decisions that had saved my life thus far, that same awareness now made every thought and feeling terrifying to me. Instead of being able to cope in some way with everything that came my way, all I felt was unmediated and absolute terror. Everything around and within me was petrifying. No self-made mediation, rationalization, or prayer was possible. Though I was covered with mud, it seemed to me as if I had no skin—nothing to separate me from the world outside of me or the emotions boiling within me.

What I experienced was beyond physical fear for my safety: it was raw fear of the Lord. I feared the Lord of the universe, the terror of the night, the power of the river, and the unforgiving rage of the water surging onto the dry land. My world had been turned upside down: the earth reeled and rocked, and the foundations of the mountains trembled and quaked. From the depths of my heart, I found the psalms of the Hebrew Bible rising from a deep place within me.

I'd been reciting the psalms each day at that point of my life for over twenty-two years. At Our Lady of Grace Monastery I'd sung all 150 of them in the choir each four-week cycle since I was eighteen years old. They were so much a part of me that in the course of my chanting over the years, the words and music had transcended their literal meaning and had deepened themselves into a comfortable dependence on the Lord.

However, what had previously been a metaphorical and spiritual testament of faith now became all too real and stark. I felt I was drowning. As with the psalmist, the waters came up to my neck, and I had sunk in a deep mire where I could find no foothold. The flood swept over me and the clouds poured out water; the crash of the thunder was in the whirlwind and God's "arrows" flashed on every side. My bones and soul shook with terror, I felt utterly spent and crushed, and I groaned because of the tumult in my heart. My bones clung to my skin, and I almost withered away like grass. My throat was parched and I was weary of crying. My strength failed me and the light of my eyes grew dim. I was asking God to come to my assistance, to make haste to help me.

I knew I couldn't save myself. Something other than me had to rescue me from this flood. Quite literally, I lifted my eyes unto the hills and stretched out my arms, pleading for God's help. "*Sanctus, sanctus, sanctus,*" I shouted at the top of my voice. "Holy, holy, holy." Again and again, one after the other, the psalms rose unbidden by my mind and flowed from me, the words echoing the pain and honesty of the psalmist all those centuries before. Like him—or perhaps her—I called for sanctuary, and like him or her I hoped against hope that the isolation, dread, and terror might be eased and I might be returned to the safety of dry land and shelter before the morning light.

At this point, of course, I'd moved far beyond whatever I may have learned exegetically about the psalms and their categories at the university—about the parallels and oppositions between or within psalms or their verses. Sometimes, I'm sure, I mixed the verses up, sometimes I put two or more psalms together, and sometimes what I cried out was a surge of pain: "Help Me!" But I was far from the recitations of Beech Grove now, far from the library of a university or cloister of a monastery, or indeed any protective shelter where I could take refuge.

Indeed, in my helplessness and in the face of the storm that was still howling around me, I was not so much praying the psalms as they were pouring out from the very marrow of my being. I feared the water coming up to my neck and prayed that I wouldn't drown. And yet—crucially—I didn't feel rebuked by God or that the violence of the storm was an expression of God's anger. Nor did I feel abandoned by God, since I knew in death that I would go to God. I wasn't asking for salvation from a position that I was chosen by God to be a servant, that I was a monastic who'd dedicated my life to God through Jesus Christ, and that I deserved some kind of special consideration because I was far from home or a woman. I wasn't praying in the mood of self-recrimination or in sorrow for any sins I'd committed, nor was I reviewing my life in contrition.

Instead, I was throwing my whole self on God's mercy and asking to be saved. I worshipped God with my head on the ground and my hands in the air. I forgave everyone whom I felt had offended me, and let go of any lingering resentments I held. I was in awe at the terror and the majesty of God, and yet drawn to God's presence and the promise of a foundation (the rock) and safety (the refuge). At that moment, I turned my life completely to God, recklessly, with total abandonment. Whatever happened would be my Lord's will, whether I survived this flood or not.

◄◄—►►

Suddenly, in the darkness on the shore of the other side of the river I saw a light, which lingered for what must have been several minutes. I tried to get to my feet. Yet the violent shaking of my legs from fear, weakness, and shock made it almost impossible for me to stand. Finally, however, I rose upright and waved the flashlight that through the grace of God I still held in my hand and still worked, flicking the switch on and off, and screaming for help.

Heartbreakingly, however, the light vanished. I wondered whether my chance of rescue had likewise disappeared when, a few minutes later, seven or eight lights appeared. As quickly as I could, I got to my feet again, and yelled and shouted—shaking the flashlight back and forth. But, once again, one by one the lights dimmed and then were gone. I found myself sitting on the mud, crying and praying. I don't recall the prayers having any other content than *help, help, help*. Sometimes, though, that's all you can ask. Again, the lights appeared, and I shouted out and waved the flashlight, and again they disappeared in the dark.

Then, to my astonishment, after what may have been a few minutes or a few hours later, but in either case seemed an age, two naked indigenous men, whose names I learned later were Oscar and Raul, emerged from the water, and walked over to me. They lifted me up, and clasped me between them. I felt the warmth of their bodies, pressed close to mine. I'd never before been so mindful of how important it is to hold someone, or be held, or so grateful that we'd found each other.

They were *campesinos*, speaking Quechua. Their bodies shook from the cold, and for a brief moment we huddled in a circle on the mudflat—three people, bound together beyond our differences of language, nationality, culture, and gender, by the simple fact that we were alive. One of them lifted his hand and stroked my cheek, trying to scrape off the mud. "*Madre, madre*," he said, tracing my face with his thumb. To this day, I don't know if he was disappointed that he hadn't found Gilchrist or Mary or Gerry—one of the nuns he would have been familiar with; but he didn't show it.

Raul and Oscar tied the rope they'd brought with them around my waist, and did the same around their own. We then stumbled up and down the flat, looking for a good place to ford the river, still swollen with mud and water and crisscrossed with currents that were treacherous. We were forced to walk upriver, just so that in the passage over we'd be able to angle ourselves with the flow to arrive at the correct place downstream where the remaining members of the rescue party were waiting. Just how difficult this was we soon discovered after we chose a place and began to make our way over. None of us was tall enough to be able to walk on the bottom of the still turbulent river; every now and again, one of the men would sink, and the other would have to drop back and pull on the rope and bring him up to the surface. I cannot recall how long it took us to cross the river, but the journey seemed to last forever. I only regret that I had so little energy with which to help my rescuers.

Finally, Oscar, Raul, and I reached the other bank, where I was lifted out of the river. I was met by Sister Rita. The local women took off my wet, muddy clothing and provided me with clean, dry garments, the same they wore for everyday living. However, because I was the same size as an indigenous man, and therefore larger than their womenfolk, the shirt wouldn't close, which meant my breasts were exposed. I didn't care. It felt so wonderful to be embraced by these people, as though they were my own family, and to be carried away from the river.

Even then, the path back to the main roadway was difficult to negotiate. Initially, the men tried to carry me on their backs, but my breathing was highly constricted, and so I asked to be helped to walk with them instead. Therefore, with men on either side of me lifting me up, we managed to stagger across a few muddy fields and walk along the railroad tracks for perhaps a couple of miles before we arrived at the team's truck, where the search party, which included Father Matt, was waiting to take us back to Charamoco.

It was midnight.

6

The Aftermath

En route to the truck, Sister Rita and Father Matt told me what had happened. A local family had seen our jeep careening down the swollen waters. The Willys had apparently hit a cement dam. When they'd seen the crash, the family had rushed back to Charamoco and had alerted Matt and Rita. But before either could get to the river, some local men had commandeered the truck and had organized a search party from Charamoco to find us. All the roads had been covered in such thick mud that the truck had been forced to travel down the railroad tracks to get closer to the mouth of the river.

My walking up and down the four mudflats that I'd negotiated out of the river had initially confused the search party. They'd seen my flashlight blinking on and off far upriver beyond where I could have been dumped from the path of the jeep. Finally, the search party had caught a glimpse of my flashlight blinking and waving on that distant mudflat, and had yelled at me as I was yelling at them. I hadn't heard them, but they'd heard me shout that I was Mary Margaret. The string of lights that I'd seen on the island in the river had consisted of torches made of rags that the search party had dowsed in kerosene, placed on sticks, and set on fire.

Rita wanted to know whether anyone else had been washed away with me. I told her *no*, and asked whether they'd found anyone.

"Gilchrist," Rita said.

"Don't tell Mary Margaret," Matt interjected. "She's in enough shock."

"Did she make it?" I asked. But I already knew the answer. In fact, while I was resting briefly on the debris in the middle of the Rio Roche, a feeling had come over me that neither Gilchrist nor the others had survived. The waters would have been too potent and beyond anyone's strength even if they'd managed to get out of the jeep, especially given that the last time I saw Gilchrist she'd been frozen with fear.

Rita shook her head. It was then I saw Gilchrist's body lying at the side of the railroad tracks. I wept. As best as could be figured out, the jeep had followed me down the *acequia* for some distance. I'd jumped shortly before the Willys had reached a railroad trestle across the concrete dam that was a trough-like conduit. I must have been swept along underneath the trestle, while the jeep had hit the bridge, and the impact had sliced off the vehicle's top, flipping it on its side and pushing it up onto one of the very high banks that flanked the *acequia*.

The search team had discovered the jeep at ten o'clock that evening. Gilchrist's hand had been sticking out of the water from the window of the Willys. Her body had been pinned in the vehicle, so the rescue party had had to wait until the waters receded slightly to be able to lift the jeep and extricate her. The Willys still had its lights on.

As Rita told me how Gilchrist had been found, my mind went back to one of her signature salutations: "Keep your taillight lit." Over the fifteen years that I knew her, Gilchrist had said it often—mostly as a gesture of farewell. I never quite understood what the phrase meant, except that it might have been a kind of scriptural pun on the wise virgins who kept their lamps burning, or an expression of hope that we should attempt to be beacons of inspiration to others. Mostly, I suppose, it was simply a way of saying, "Take care!" Or how the Irish say, "Mind yourself." Certainly, that I'd kept the flashlight in my hand throughout my whole time was a miracle—even as I'd tried to give it away to Juanito; especially, since the other, smaller flashlight that I had on my person had become clogged with mud and no longer functioned. Perhaps I had indeed kept my taillight lit.

Although the coroner's report stated that Gilchrist drowned, it's my belief that she probably died from concussion when the jeep hit the railroad bridge. To my relief, Gilchrist's countenance appeared peaceful and without tension. When I remembered the stony look on her face, her halting words about the danger we found ourselves in, and how the care for Juanito among the three nuns was greater than concern for their own safety, it was evident to me that none of them grasped just how serious the situation was. And that, in its own way, may have been a blessing.

I also learned that, after I was discovered, Father Matt and the large rescue party were forced to give up the effort because the night was too dark and the roads too muddy. It was still raining and in many places the waters were continuing to rise. The members of the local search party were putting themselves at great risk. Matt, however, without the search party, went back out to try to find Jack, who'd gone to the nearest house soon after jumping from the jeep.

Gilchrist's eyes were still open, so I closed them. I offered a prayer, as my way of saying *goodbye* to her and commending her to God's loving mercy. The men from the search party loaded Gilchrist's body into the truck, and drove us back to the house in Charamoco, from which we'd set out only a few hours—but now a lifetime—before. The men laid Gilchrist out on the dining-room table. Matt and Rita knelt and said prayers for the dying that commend a soul to God. They placed me in a sleeping bag on a bed in the other room and

Rita put a butterfly bandage over my closed eye to stop the bleeding and close the wound. She then left me to tend to Gilchrist's body.

I hurt from head to toe. I was in shock: my breath came in pants, and I barely knew where the next one was coming from. I lay wide-awake with my one good eye staring at the ceiling. I didn't want the light in my room turned out, because light now seemed very precious to me, as did the company of people. Then I heard Father Matt's voice from the next room.

"Is she going to make it?" he asked Rita.

"No," she replied.

Given that I was the only person in the building who was still alive, I realized they were talking about me. I felt terrible. Rita was the medical specialist on the team, so I assumed she knew what she was talking about. *After all that effort and trauma*, I thought, *I'm going to die anyway*.

It seemed useless to take care of myself, so I lifted myself from the bed and shuffled into the dining room, the sleeping bag still around my legs and feet. Rita was sitting on the side bench, weeping beside Gilchrist's body, which was now covered with a clean, white sheet, with a lit candle on each side of her head. When Rita saw me, she welcomed me to the opposite bench beside the table that was serving as Gilchrist's bier. Rita made and served two Manhattans, and we took our positions, one on either side of Gilchrist's body. We told stories, cried, and together prayed the psalms using a breviary until dawn.

I think we helped each other. Rita had known me for less than two weeks. She wanted to hear how I'd become acquainted with Gilchrist and what her colleague was like when she was younger. I told her that Gilchrist and I had been co-workers and friends; that although we'd gone our separate ways, we'd never lost touch, as some confidantes do over time. I shared with Rita that Gilchrist and I had had a great appreciation for each other, and that Gilchrist had been an enormous blessing for me after my rocky years in monastic formation.

For her part, Rita probably knew the "missioner Gilchrist" better than I did. She told me that, for the last few years, Gilchrist had become a blessed gift for her in the demanding and potentially isolating work they undertook together in Bolivia. Now she was gone, and in violent and tragic circumstances. In some ways, I felt more keenly Rita's pain at her loss than I did for the departure of my friend. For Rita, Gilchrist's death was raw and real. Ultimately, I was to return to my home in Indiana and resume life at the monastery in Beech Grove; Rita's whole mission life in Bolivia had been turned upside down in one night.

◄◄··►►

Sometime during the night, the rain finally stopped and dawn broke on a gray and overcast day, with a steady, chilly breeze. Father Matt rang the church bells for the men of the village to resume their search for the missing passengers of the wrecked jeep. Soon enough, they found the body of Juanito. Not far from him was Gerry. When Rita saw Juanito's limp and lifeless form, she simply wept. Gerry's neck and back had been broken, and it was clear from the angle of one of her arms who'd finally gotten hold of Juanito.

Judging by the water in his lungs, Juanito himself seems to have inhaled one large breath underwater and drowned. I was actually relieved that Juanito had died at the same time as Gilchrist, for I'm sure that he simply wouldn't have been able to continue to thrive without her. As it happened, he passed away with all these women whom he loved, and who loved him, and who loved each other. They were the best of friends.

The men from the search party brought in Juanito and Gerry's bodies. Rita and the devout local women cleaned them up, and then put fresh, dry clothes on them. By that time, *campesinos* were emerging from the nearby mountains and foothills—a steady flow of people walking up from the village and converging on the house. They wailed and greeted us and then stood in total silence as we went about dealing with the bodies. At first, their quiet was unnerving, but it became evident that it was a mark of the profoundest respect and deepest grief. They had loved the *madrecitas*—or "little mothers"—who'd taken such care of them, and with whom they'd shared their burdens and hospitality. The *madrecitas* had likewise mourned the *campesinos'* own losses—losses that in their difficult and tenuous existence in the mountains they were all too familiar with.

Because there were no telephones in the Maryknoll house nor in Charamoco, we wrote a message that was taken to the train that would pass through the village on its journey to Cochabamba. While we waited for Mary's body to be found, we gathered Gilchrist and Gerry's things together for the funeral.

As I went through Gilchrist's little room in the village house where she lived with Gerry, I was struck by what few items she possessed. I always knew Gilchrist lived simply, but I'd never known *how* simply. Though she stored some clothes at Casa Rosario, all Gilchrist owned that needed to be returned to Chicago could fit in a doctor's bag: her flute and her Bible. She had two pairs of the jeans and sweaters that she wore almost every day, and a couple of blouses. Rita placed Gilchrist's one item of formal wear—a cherry-red suit with a nice blouse—in a bag to use for the funeral showing.

That Gilchrist had so few belongings was not a statement of her commitment to her beliefs, it was a *consequence* of her unself-conscious generosity and wholehearted love of those she'd come to serve—the people of Charamoco—and through them, Jesus Christ. She wasn't a willful ascetic:

she enjoyed laughter and music, the Manhattans and a good feast. Nor was she naïve or overly idealistic about the challenges that faced her and the others as they carried out their tasks in Bolivia. However, in her dedication to the poor and the absolute simplicity with which she lived, she had truly internalized the Gospels, and her attitude to life and the passion she brought to her work came from a place of abiding consciousness of God's love. She always had more to give because God replenished the joy in her heart.

It was clear that we had to return to Cochabamba. I required medical attention—I was running a fever—and the bodies needed utmost respect and proper burial according to each one's customs and community traditions. Father Matt and his search party were also still looking for Mary (whose body, as it turned out, was found eight miles downstream and was taken back to Cochabamba soon after). By 11:30 a.m., however, it became too late to wait for Matt and the second search party, as the little house was filling up with mourners.

Some men from the village then loaded the bodies of Gilchrist, Gerry, and Juanito onto the back of truck. (Father Jack, who'd arrived at the house earlier that morning needing attention for a jammed index finger, was also in the rear.) Lifting the dead bodies was as solemn as any graveside ritual, and the local men accomplished this with great deliberation. Rita drove and I took the passenger seat. My awareness was greatly heightened as I scanned the water-soaked terrain and the many streams crisscrossing the road. Because of the size of the truck, we were able to cross a river that only fifteen hours before we had been trapped in. Nonetheless, I could see that it was still wild and swollen, and had spilled into the nearby cornfields. I recall that on the other side of the town of Charamoco a group of men selflessly hitched a ride on the truck for about two or three miles to inspect the river and help Rita judge if it was safe to ford. Once they'd declared it was, they walked back to town.

There was a toll booth on the highway when we turned onto the main road back toward Cochabamba. Rita decided not to stop the truck as she just wasn't up to dealing with inquiries about the bodies. This proved to be a mistake as later she and Father Jack had to explain to Bolivian authorities that there'd been no foul play in the accident. It certainly helped that the sheriff of Charamoco had been part of the rescue party.

We traveled to St. Vincent's Hospital, then owned and staffed by the Daughters of Charity, where I got attention for my face wounds and received infusions of fluids. The Superior, Sister Elizabeth Berry, sibling of the famous theologian and ecologist Father Thomas Berry, showed us the utmost hospitality and kindness. She took charge to make sure proper refrigeration and embalming for the bodies were available and that I received good medical care. She and her nuns even organized the wake services.

Because it was a Sunday, however, these tasks were harder to accomplish than on any other day of the week. Cochabamba only had two coroners. One was on vacation, while the other refused to work on the day of rest. It took an intervention from the bishop of Cochabamba to accomplish all the legal details so that the bodies were released for the proper burial rituals. After a brief stay in hospital, I was taken to Casa Rosario, where Liz, a Maryknoll Sister and a seasoned nurse, looked after me until I recovered enough to fly home.

<-<-->->

Before I returned to the United States, I attended two funerals. The first was for Juanito. We traveled to the house of Doña Blanca, who'd taken great care of Juanito's little body, and we held a service in their home. We shared songs, testimonies, and prayers around the casket, which although it had openings for the head, body, and feet, was only open for the head. We then climbed into our jeeps and drove to the Cochabamba cemetery. Although I was scarcely able to walk, I wanted to be present for Juanito and to honor his short but significant life.

The cemetery consisted of mausoleums and tombs neatly placed one on top of the other. Sister Rita had bought a burial space for Juanito. We placed his casket in the open vault, and I watched as a man arrived with a wheelbarrow full of bricks and mortar and began to seal it up. In one of our late-night conversations only a few days before, I'd asked Gilchrist what she'd do with Juanito when she returned to the United States in two years at the end of her mission—given that her attempt to have him adopted by her brother and his wife seemed very unlikely to happen. Gilchrist told me that she wasn't too concerned because Rita had promised to take care of him. I remembered these sentiments as Rita wrote Juanito's name with her finger in the wet cement of his tomb. Rita had fulfilled her promise.

At the moment when Juanito's vault was almost completely sealed, I turned and looked behind me. To my astonishment, as far as the eye could see, children of all ages had crowded into the cemetery and were lined up all the way down the street, standing to attention in respectful silence. It was as if every child in Cochabamba had turned out to say *goodbye* to the little orphan boy who was lame, mute, and partially deaf. Juanito Vargas, in his brief life, had filled everyone with joy.

The second funeral was the following day, at the Old Spanish cathedral in Cochabamba. It poured with rain. At the altar in the cathedral were laid the three caskets for Mary, Gilchrist, and Gerry. Rita suggested that the two priests, Matt and Jack, remain with her and me and not vest and concelebrate with the other priests. Gilchrist, she said, wouldn't have approved and, in any case, it was important symbolically for us to stay together. To their credit, Matt and Jack agreed, which took courage, because they would have been expected to officiate at the altar with the fifty other priests instead of sitting in the front pew with us. In attendance were hundreds of missioners—from Ireland, England, Peru, Ecuador, and from all regions of Bolivia—who'd gathered for a more joyous occasion. Also assembled were the students who'd been commissioned as catechists the previous Sunday. In all, the congregation numbered about a thousand or more, many of them *campesinos*.

In his homily, one of the five bishops presiding over the service mentioned that the first time he'd encountered the team of four nuns and two priests, he'd been skeptical of what they were attempting to accomplish. There was, he said, no precedent for such a team approach in this vast rural region of his Archdiocese. However, the second time he'd met them on-site, he'd seen that their ways were working; and this time he was convinced that their methods were exceptional. That day, he challenged the congregation to conduct their mission outreach the same way as this team. He offered a moving tribute to Gerry, Gilchrist, and Mary, and all the American missioners in Bolivia, about how they'd traveled from the richest country in the world to one of the poorest, and had given their all, even to the point of losing their lives.

On each of the three coffins, servers had placed an *aguayo*. The bishop entrusted Rita, Matt, and me with the task of taking one *aguayo* back to each of the families, along with their bodies. Rita was to accompany Gerry's body to New York; two of the Dominicans who lived in Bolivia were to bring Mary's body to Dubuque; and I was to take Gilchrist's body back to Chicago and give the *aguayo* to her mother, Julia.

After the service, the congregation crowded around us and extended their sympathy. At first I resisted. I'd only been in the country a few days, and I felt awkward at being the recipient of the warmth and love they poured out. But then I relented and accepted that the local people weren't only blessing me, but were extending their love to all those who'd been lost and the hope they represented to these people in their faith. To the Bolivians it was a miracle that someone had lived through the storm, and they were overwhelmed. It was not about me; I understood the message to be that the people saw my preservation as a manifestation of our shared faith in Christ.

They gave me a beautiful shawl, which I treasure to this day. In response, I found myself speaking understandable Spanish—or something that passed for Spanish—to the astonished group. In fact, one Maryknoll sister said, "I didn't know you could speak Spanish." And I couldn't, and I still can't. I was, however, still in such a state of shock that I was probably in effect speaking in tongues rather than communicating in a known language. Of course, I should just say, *I don't know how I did it, but by the grace of God, I did.*

Even in my heightened state, I could see that the church was full of tearful mourners celebrating the life of those three nuns and one orphan boy, and that by the numbers of people at the funeral and the depth of their grief, the sisters had been very dear to the community. Perhaps the manner of their deaths also contributed to these feelings. The three may have been ill-advised and impetuous in setting off that evening and in such weather, but the decision had been made from zeal rather than negligence, and that had struck a chord with everybody. They'd taken the risk because they wanted to serve others.

The funeral gathering of friends continued until ten o'clock that evening. At Casa Rosario, Rita and other Maryknoll Sisters rose at 4:30 the next morning and prepared an enormous feast for thirty or more people. They cooked beans, potatoes, dressing, gravy, and, of all things, the turkey that I'd brought from the U.S., and which had remained in Cochabamba the entire time. The missioners, the Maryknoll priests, the Dominicans, the three survivors of the team, and I then gathered in the large dining room of Casa Rosario, and ate. We sang songs and drank Manhattans and made toasts to our now deceased sisters and the beautiful child, Juanito.

My injuries aside, I knew it was more than time for me to go home to Indiana. Too much had occurred, and I needed a deeper rest to get over the shock of what had happened. The next day, a huge group of people—priests, peasants, the mechanic of Rita's blue jeep, and others—brought drums and accompanied us to the airport.

We still had a great deal of red tape to cut through associated with the passports, the coroner's report, and the removal of the three caskets from the country. However, a few days after the funeral we were at last settled on the plane. Following a long layover in Santa Cruz and many other airports, I arrived back in Chicago with Gilchrist's body. At the gate to meet me were my father, dressed in his best suit; my oldest brother, Jim; my older sister, Evelyn; Sister Mary Sue; Sister Carol; and many nuns from Beech Grove, which was 250 miles away. Meeting Gilchrist's brother Tommy was the saddest encounter of my whole life, even to this day. I gave him the official papers with which he could negotiate the handover of Gilchrist's body from O'Hare Airport authorities to the funeral directors.

The wake was on Thursday and Friday, and on Saturday morning at St. Barnabas church in Chicago a beautiful funeral was held for Gilchrist. Many Bolivians living in Chicago came to pay their respects and mourn with us. I then returned to Beech Grove on a Greyhound bus with Sister Mary Sue, as my Benedictine nuns could not stay in Chicago for all the rituals surrounding Gilchrist's burial. I was picked up at the bus station in Indianapolis and driven to Our Lady of Grace Monastery.

It was three degrees below zero Fahrenheit when our

car pulled in. To my stunned amazement, all the nuns, from the oldest to the youngest, were lined up to welcome me at the back door as I greeted them one by one. Sister Geraldine, the oldest, was first to extend her arms and embrace me. Then followed Sister Rosina, Sister Scholastica, Sister Mary Robert, Sister Valeria, Sister Helen Wagner, and on through the tens of other dear sisters. I have no idea what I said, or what was spoken to me, or if any words were uttered at all. But as I made my way down the long hall of Our Lady of Grace, I felt deeply touched, both inside and out.

I was home.

◄◄--►►

No one should have lived through that night. The water was too strong and too deep, and I fell too far into that major river, then at flood stage, for me to survive. I might have been able to react more quickly than others to the danger posed as the jeep began to float. I may have had the skills developed all those years before at high school in being able to swim. I may have had the forethought to carry a flashlight to find my way. But I knew then—as I am certain to this day—that it was only through the grace of God that I survived.

I was to discover later that, in addition to the rain that had swelled the normally passable streams that crisscrossed the road to Cochabamba, the rain had also overflowed a lake further up in the mountains, causing the cascade that fell through the region to be that much stronger. Because the area had been undergoing a drought, the ground was also rock hard and thus unable to absorb fast enough the huge amount of rain that fell in such a short space of time. As to the *acequia* in which we got stuck, it was suggested to me later that a natural dam high above us in the mountains must have broken its banks due to the rains, and the other waterways that were normally dry ravines had opened and had channeled a large amount of water through this particular conduit.

The three nuns and Juanito were not the only victims of the storm. Some of the houses of Charamoco's villagers were swept away. Each year the Andes mountains claim many lives because of swollen rivers and landslides. And yet, I had been spared, rescued, and had now returned home.

Two months later—March 27, 1984—I received a letter from Sister Rita:

> Yesterday I went on a pilgrimage down the riverbed. I was shocked. It was much longer than I had imagined. Many more turns; overhanging branches—Most of all there is no human way that you could have passed the railroad bridge without getting smashed to pieces—no way. Again after the bridge, the mouth of the

river was much farther than I had imagined. This probably doesn't make sense—but it was much further—much more hazardous and more miraculous that you are alive—than I had imagined. . . .

PART III

The Response

7

Out of the Depths

The incident in Bolivia washed out of me any further desire for academia that I might have had. It also signaled that—Manhattans and bridge games aside—the life of a missioner was not my calling. After I returned to the U.S., I taught summer school at St. Meinrad Seminary and in the fall I was assigned work in the Archdiocese of Louisville, Kentucky, as an adult education coordinator. I worked under Bishop Thomas Kelly and lived with ten other nuns from Beech Grove at St. Anthony's convent in Clarksville, near Louisville. Twice a day I commuted over the Interstate 65 bridge across the Ohio River, and observed the mood of that river through fall, winter, spring, and summer. It was strangely healing to pass over the wide river safely each morning and evening with the other thousands of cars. At night in my dreams I'd see that arched steel construction in ever-changing forms.

In March 1985, I was elected the prioress of Our Lady of Grace, a position that I held until 1993. In 1989, I was invited onto the board of Monastic Interreligious Dialogue (MID), ultimately becoming its executive director. MID is an organization founded by the Vatican to sponsor dialogue between Catholic monks and nuns and their fellow monastics in the Buddhist and Hindu traditions, although many monastics, including myself, have also engaged in interreligious dialogue with Jews and Muslims as well. Throughout this time, up until the present, I was writing and teaching.

Such are the broad outlines of my life following my return to the U.S. in January 1984. However, my interior life was considerably more full of turmoil than the details of my outer life would suggest. I did, indeed, recover relatively quickly from the physical wounds I'd acquired the night of the flood. Even though to this day I still have a scar on my face from my collision with the tree-branch, the surgeon stitched up the wound skillfully and professionally. Likewise, the marks from the insects' pincers and the serrations of the pampas grass have long since healed.

Although for two years I was bothered with internal physical ailments—mainly in the form of sprained wrists and ankles and muscle spasms in my back and face—all these injuries eventually vanished.

The trauma experienced by the deeper nervous tissues of

my body and the neurons of my brain, however, was something no surgeon could stitch up. On the face of it, all was fine. Only a few days after returning from burying Gilchrist, I gave two presentations to the local monastic community about what happened. When I listen today to the audiotapes that were made of my talks, I sound like a different person, my voice slightly raised in pitch and with a detached tone that masks all but a few moments where the weight of what happened pokes through. It's the voice of someone clearly in shock. I hadn't yet mentally processed the fact that one of my dearest friends had died, two other nuns and a little orphan boy had lost their lives, and that I myself had been taken to the very extremes of fear and exhaustion. Somehow, as I relate the tale, it is all for the greater glory of God.

My subconscious, however, wouldn't let me return to my former way of life as if nothing had happened. In the weeks and months after my return from Bolivia, I remained extremely sensitive to cold. Loud noises—the thrumming of rain on a roof, the howling of the wind, the sound of rushing water—were amplified in my head beyond all tolerance. No matter how hard I tried, I couldn't rationalize away the feeling that I wasn't once again on the river, being eaten alive by insects, or shouting out for help.

The trauma invaded my dreams. I found myself falling over and over again into the Rio Roche: my face pressed against the moss-covered rocks, my body sliding down and down, my hands trying to grip and hold on, and then failing and tumbling over the slippery surfaces into the river. Repeatedly, I'd be pulled beneath the surface and then struggle up for air. And gruesome images filled these dreams. Instead of dead cattle and uprooted trees being swept along in the current, human bodies floated with me down the river.

Periodically, I would experience panic attacks, which would usually occur when I was driving in the rain, either by myself or with someone else. My nerves would act as if I were back in the Rio Roche. Not surprisingly perhaps, these episodes would often happen when I traveled through mountainous areas. Two years after I returned from Bolivia in 1986, I visited Our Lady of Grace's mission in Colombia. On the drive between Cali and Cartagena, as our jeep crossed the mountains, my breath suddenly became short, every muscle tensed, my heart began to beat as though it would explode from my chest, and sweat started to pour from me.

On another occasion, in Ogden, Utah, a group of nuns I was staying with wanted to visit the Cistercian monks at the Abbey of Our Lady of the Holy Trinity, which is situated amid spectacular mountain scenery in Huntsville, sixteen miles away across Ogden Canyon. Normally, I would have enjoyed such a trip, since I used to love hiking in the mountains of Colorado. However, I immediately felt dread creeping over me. I told those who were to journey with me that I didn't want to go on the excursion—perhaps unconsciously reflecting my similar reluctance to travel that night to Cochabamba. "Oh yes, you do," they said, equally unconsciously mimicking Gilchrist's dismissal of my concern. "It's only a few minutes," they added. Except that it wasn't a few minutes, just like it wasn't only a shower that night in January 1984. At least, not to me. Every minute felt like an hour as we drove through the mountains of the Wasatch-Cache National Forest.

These attacks didn't necessarily require mountains or rain to spring their surprises. I remember attending the board meeting of the Weston School of Theology in Cambridge, Massachusetts, and being forced to leave because the level of functioning required for the meeting suddenly extended beyond my ability. I was obliged to stay with my sister Carolyn in New Jersey until I could recover my strength enough to fly home. Unlike the period of depression in 1968–69, I could continue to function at my assignments throughout this period. However, my former, confident self had been replaced by an anxious mortal with abiding fatigue.

I tried every method to still the noise and reduce the trauma. I returned to therapy with a psychiatrist. I took anxiety medications, although I didn't remain on them for more than a month, because I didn't like how they made me feel either edgy or sluggish. Nowadays, of course, such episodes of panic, unease, sense of fear, and feelings of suffocation or claustrophobia are often diagnosed as symptoms of Post-

Traumatic Stress Disorder or PTSD. However, in the early 1980s, PTSD was not clearly understood; nor, even today, is "curing" such a condition an easy task.

Indeed, while I've certainly progressed in coping with the PTSD, it can still be generated in unforeseen ways. When, in December 2004, an earthquake in the Indian Ocean triggered a tsunami that took hundreds of thousands of lives in Indonesia, Thailand, Sri Lanka, and as far away as the east coast of Africa, I was devastated. Beyond a natural sympathy one might have for those who suddenly lost their lives in the midst of great beauty, I felt completely connected to the suffering of those who were swept away in the flood or left exposed to the elements. As much as I attempted to avoid the television replays of the scenes of devastation, I couldn't help reliving the fear of what it was like to be picked up, with little warning or hope of rescue, by surges of water and thrown beneath the surface of the roiling torrent. It was as if my survival instincts immediately short-circuited any rational directive my mind might give, and my emotions prompted the body to act as if it was still in danger, even though these events were many thousands of miles away.

It takes a long time to retrain the inner mechanisms of the mind and body to trust safety and security, as each cell must be consoled and gently relaxed into a normal consciousness. I also feel that diagnoses of PTSD have almost lost their gravity, and that we forget how frightening and disabling the condition is to bear. In fact, most people still imagine that the best remedy for a traumatic event is to "get over it," to "get back on the saddle," and that if one only faced the fear it would go away. However, facing a trauma head-on can often just retraumatize the nervous system rather than normalizing it. Indeed, it is my understanding that the new injury can be worse than the original wound.

That said, I certainly don't blame people for looking to the future rather than dwelling on the tragic past. At Gilchrist's funeral at St. Barnabas in Chicago, Gilchrist's younger sister, Carol Conway, told us that Gilchrist would want us to move on with our lives, and I could indeed resonate with that directive. When I thought of Rita, the Maryknoll Sisters, and the archbishop in Cochabamba who performed extraordinarily bravely and dynamically throughout the whole ordeal, and who together took care of everything, I was (and remain) in awe at the strength and conviction that carried them through. By the grace of God, I too made it through the days immediately after the deaths.

However, as time went on, I found it harder and harder either to be strong or to "move on." I was overwhelmed by a fatigue that extended beyond the healing balms of sleep or the stillness of meditation, and that felt worse than death because it consisted of the full weight of the burden of being alive when others had died. I was a trained lifeguard and had had a few incidents in my teenage life where I had plunged into the water and saved a potential drowning victim. After Bolivia, I had recurring fantasies that I could have similarly rescued Juanito and the three nuns with moves that I'd seen in films or read about in dramatic books of heroics. I regretted that I, an Indiana farm girl, hadn't been better prepared for traveling in Bolivia or that I hadn't insisted more vigorously that all of us should have stayed with Rita and Matt and gone to Mass in Charamoco that Saturday night, rather than try to drive to Cochabamba in weather that was already showing signs of becoming a major storm.

Many persons close to the accident in Bolivia told me I was experiencing "survivor's guilt"—the sense of culpability that plays out the harm done to the victims on the survivors, and twists the grief of loss into a grief at being saved. But this observation, no matter how well-intentioned it might have been, only bracketed and reduced the experience, as if simply naming something a condition could somehow heal it or contain it safely. Or it provided others with a comfortable assignation to explain what they considered to be irrational or abnormal behavior.

What hurt me more than the physical and emotional scars that I carried with me from that night was my inability to explain the depth of what I'd gone through to others, perhaps because in some ways so much of the event was beyond words. I admit that in my early attempts to explain my experience that night, I'd find myself curtailing or leaving out parts of the story, because I was overly sensitive at how the person or audience listening to the story would react.

When I tried to tell some people what had happened, I found that they'd quickly segue from it to talk about climate change or point out to me how it reminded them of some book or movie or TV reality show. Or they'd express amazement that I hadn't "gotten over it," or was still clinging to something that had happened so long ago. While over the years I did receive genuine attentiveness and a connection could be made between me and the person to whom I was telling the story, it was rare to find a listener who grasped the impact the flood had on my soul. It was as if no one had the capacity to receive what I might call the *weight* of it—that the awesome and terrible beauty of God had left me with heightened sensitivity.

When I think of the Quechuan people's alternate keening and eerie silence for the *mamacitas* they lost, how deeply reverential and present they were to the experience of death, I couldn't help but be disappointed at this reaction. The attempt to relate my own feelings taught me that people are disconnected to the reality of other people's experiences. It also showed me that we need to place a lot more trust in the way other people communicate what happens to them, both internally and externally. Sometimes, it's not enough to say you "get it," as if anyone's story is a crossword puzzle that needs to be solved. So, rather like an autistic child who struggles to express their needs, I simply went inside myself and didn't talk about what happened for ten years.

-<-<-->->-

What made the story especially difficult to communicate was that amidst the trauma I'd had a spiritual awakening. After I was pulled out of the Rio Roche, my mind felt pure and full of light. I'd forgiven everyone and everything, and believed I'd been forgiven in turn. I'd been re-baptized and was, as it were, in a wholly new place—both literally, in that I had no idea where I was, and metaphorically, in that the comforts of my previous spiritual existence had been stripped from me and I was left with only my naked faith in God. I felt utterly embraced and enveloped in God. I not only could feel people's pain with an intensity that went beyond my own suffering or ordinary empathy, but the sense of being saved spiritually was almost too much to bear. Amidst the fear of annihilation and my beseeching of the Lord, I at once rejoiced at the experience of refuge and shelter, in the sanctuary of God.

The Easter after the accident I found myself overwhelmed by the symbols of resurrection. The movement from darkness to light was enhanced by the intimate embrace of Life in all its manifestations. The smell of the lilies was intoxicating and I felt that I myself was the extinguished taper as the Easter candle plunged into the baptismal waters. In the Spring 1984 edition of the Beech Grove magazine *Encounter*, I wrote about my experiences using the *Exultet* ("O happy fault, [*felix culpa*], O necessary sin of Adam, which gained for us so great a Redeemer!"), which is sung during the Easter Mass and expresses our joy at being redeemed:

> It is truly right
> that with full hearts and minds and voices
> we should praise the unseen God,
> the powerful Breath of Life in all the living
> and our brother Jesus Christ.
>
> For it was three months ago tonight
> waters between Charamoco and Cochabamba, Bolivia,
> reclaimed the lives of four confessors.
>
> . . .
>
> That night of January 21, 1984 truly blessed,
> "when heaven wedded
> to earth, and we were reconciled with God!"
>
> Accept this Easter candle . . .
> Let it mingle with the lights of heaven

and continue bravely burning

to dispel the darkness of this night!

I'm well aware now that some might argue that these religious feelings were merely further symptoms of PTSD— that I was already in distress over my failure at Catholic University of America and in a heightened emotional state, and that what happened in Bolivia pushed me over the edge. Certainly, I can recognize in my writing at Easter 1984 residues of the shock from just a few months earlier. In my personal engagement with therapists over forty years I've seen the value of deepening my understanding of patterns of behavior and recognizing at least in part the neurological and biochemical roots of depression.

That said, I can't reduce the *spiritual* crises of 1968 and Catholic U. in 1983 to mere psychological reflex or unprocessed emotion—because such reductivism would be profoundly untrue to the nature of this experience. Nor can I dismiss as *merely* survivor's guilt or delayed PTSD the inner flood that was the aftermath of my encounter both above and beneath the river, and which is the subject of the next chapter. In fact, the real crisis was just beginning, and I found myself totally unprepared for how far down the inner waters would pull me.

8

Falling into the Arms of God

The pure point of connection between the human and divine that I'd experienced blissfully under the river in Bolivia didn't save me from further troubles when I returned to the U.S. in January 1984. If the story of the accident and my experience underneath the river was difficult to put in words, it was virtually impossible to share what I came to see as a second, inner flood that also washed through me. Unlike the exterior storm, this particular flood would rise from time to time and overwhelm me in such a way that my life felt in even more danger than that night in Bolivia. These waters didn't cascade down the mountainsides; they welled up and flooded my own soul.

The question I'd asked as a child of three—*Which is truly real, inside or outside?*—came back to haunt me. This time, however, it took another form: *If God is so good, then why do I feel so bad?* Unlike in 1968, what weighed me down was not my very existence, but the full burden of my own presence. In the 1970s I'd felt on fire with the Holy Spirit guiding me and working through me. After the flood, I felt keenly how raw and unclothed my very *human* being was.

This feeling was quantifiably different from the shot nerves, hyperventilation, or hypothermia that affected my physical body. It was a kind of self-consciousness, far more stifling than the oppressive formation I'd undergone in the novitiate. My ego demanded attention far beyond normal drives toward competition or public acclaim. Leaping off the jeep; sinking down into the rushing waters saturated with mud; banging into trees, pampas grass, and rocks; rapids and flesh-eating insects—all these were one thing. But the hyper-consciousness that rose from my interior waters felt much more serious. In other words, I was literally so full of myself that it was unbearable. In such a situation, there were no easy solutions for anger or depression. Changing my schedule or where I lived or what I worked at, or acquiring another superior or a different set of obligations, would be futile. I simply couldn't avoid taking myself with me!

Jean-Paul Sartre famously said that hell is other people. My experience, however, is that hell is absolute self-absorption. Turning all talk and otherness back toward my judgmental and fiercely self-centered being was the opposite of my previous encounters with God that had led to me bowing down to the ground and lifting my eyes in supplication. I was overly sensitive to everything, keenly aware of how I felt about others. Psychiatry or counseling, or any medical or psychotropic remedies, may have been able to calm the surface of my body and anesthetize my mind, but they simply didn't touch my soul. They didn't provide me with ways to deal with the irritation or anger I felt at everyone who didn't respond appropriately to my wants or who acted in ways that I felt were dishonorable and didn't accord with their vows.

The healing modalities didn't stop the incessant chatter— the internal bickering with myself and others, the sniping critiques and ever-present annoyance that would accumulate until I'd created characters, drama, and vivid coloration that bore little relation to the situation to which I'd initially reacted. I'd imagine scenes where I'd confront the individual, full of righteous fury; I'd obsess over the details of how somebody somewhere had made a mistake or underperformed, and how I would have done everything better.

The distorted prism of my own ego didn't allow me to see straight. Any anger I didn't resolve turned into a generalized bad mood and then a long, lingering depression that took the form of an undifferentiated sadness about everyone and everything, with no content or story line. Now, it's true that sometimes my emotional state reflected a real wrong; but the reality was overlaid with an all-consuming anger that made an appropriate reaction impossible. All that happened was further aggravation. Although I seldom acted out on this anger, the simmering irritation or annoyance might last an hour, a day, a couple of months, or (in the case of my response to one particular individual) for two years.

My anger was directed at many things: I was angry that those of us in the jeep hadn't responded to the situation and simply stopped before we'd reached the river or evacuated the vehicle before it was too late. I was angry that no one had listened to my trepidation, expressed many times. I was also angry at Jack for jumping into the darkness and leaving us. It was clear to me that the choices he made weren't the only ones that could have been made.

Yet I would be dishonest if I didn't acknowledge that anger is in its way a *comforting* emotion. As much as it may come from genuine pain and have a just cause, it can also be a way of numbing deeper and more complicated feelings— such as guilt, vulnerability, and loss—that aren't so easily blamed on an outside source or individual.

For in the end, I don't know why Jack jumped and fled. He had his reasons, and he told me some of them. But the feelings that lay behind those reasons are opaque—perhaps even to him. What I can be sure of is that whatever his version of the events of January 21, 1984, I can only be responsible for mine. And I cannot deny that Jack was not the only one who jumped that night. In fact, it was because he left the door of the Willys open that I was able to climb onto the roof and be in a position to leap from the jeep, and thus save my life.

I also felt vainglory—an inordinate pride not only at my own accomplishments, but in the greatness that was Me! Ironically, this affliction manifested itself in my clamoring for attention and pursuing tasks and goals that would give me the glory and renown I sought, and exhaust me so much that I could be a martyr at the same time. I experienced years of fatigue, unable to judge how much was too much, how long was too long, or how heavy was too heavy—because everything was too much, too long, and too heavy. I traveled, studied, planned, administered, taught, and counseled with a kind of mania that meant I frequently fell ill, slept at every possible opportunity, and yet never felt well or rested.

I made no distinction between my own inner contemplative work, community responsibilities, and optional outside activities. I tried to do everything, because everything seemed maximally worthy and important, and I was the best person to do it. I traveled as much as I could, and found myself not only gone from home, but gone from myself. The fatigue kept warning me that such freneticism was unsustainable, but in the wake of Bolivia I thought this craziness was, in some perverse way, a gift.

What fueled me was not only a desire I had to please myself, but to have the men and women for and with whom I worked reflect the considerable pride that I felt in myself. I not only disregarded the opinions and contribution of others, but I paid no attention to the God-given graces that come from humility, except when I failed. I should say that just as my anger reflected in some cases a real situation, so some of my achievements were real and lasting; the work was good and blessed by God. But what I forgot was that this was not "the work" that God was asking me to do: *that* lay in the rounds of prayer, monastic routine, and spiritual cultivation that were very healthy for me, and which I neglected at my peril.

Throughout this time, I knew deep down that, in spite of the diagnoses I received of depression and grief due to the trauma of loss, these emotional bouts were too thick and entrenched to be cured by talk therapy or medication. Nor would blind obedience, intellectual discipline, or willpower school them.

Simply trying to do good and avoiding evil would never be enough to make them go away. I needed stronger methods to strengthen my aching soul, and to understand what felt more like a sacred wound than something to do with my emotional limitations. I required something to redirect the ego-sourced thoughts and emotions that caused me to be so self-centered. I longed for ceaseless prayer that promotes stillness of body, mind, and spirit; I wanted to return to that presence of myself that was pure under the river.

The former spiritual graces of being nothing at St. Vincent's Hospital and longing for God at CUA simply got covered over. The Bolivian waters washed me clean but a deeper sludge mired my ego and fixated my consciousness toward the self. Would I need yet another life-threatening crisis to save me? Again, I sought help.

<del>-<-+->-</del>

What finally became my rock of safety in the vast roiling inner river that rushed through my core was what had been before me the entire time: my vocation as a nun. When I was elected the prioress in 1985, I started teaching the *Rule of Benedict*, which I'd memorized as a young novice. In the process of learning more deeply about the *Rule*, however, I discovered to my amazement that the sources that Benedict had drawn upon were unfamiliar to me. Over the forty years of my education in my faith, I'd studied more about the Church and its traditions than the monastic traditions themselves. To my delight and incredulity, I found a treasure trove of wisdom in the teachings of the monastic elders that Benedict in his genius had gathered to form the *Rule*.

It's astonishing to think that much of what is now considered essential reading for the monastic life was, in the early 1980s, only available in part, and then mostly in Latin, French, or Spanish.

The Christian monastic life had its origins in Egypt, Syria, and Palestine in the fourth and fifth centuries. At that time, men and women decided to pursue and deepen their faith by moving into the desert and living in solitude and prayer. By relocating to the stark and unsparing climate of the desert, these individuals assumed that they'd be saved from the temptations of living in the world and would be able to cultivate what they called *apatheia*, which is not a condition of indifference but can be translated as "equanimity," or what Benedict calls "purity of heart." They felt that simple separation from the world and a pared-down life would provide suitable circumstances for a close relationship with God. Such assumptions still color our views of monastic life today.

The Elders discovered, however, that no matter how far they fled into the desert and or how intently they practiced their austerities, the demands of their inner selves were much more daunting obstacles to *apatheia* than any of the external physical or natural forces they had encountered. In the silence of their cells and without the distractions of the outer world, the Elders were often confronted not with the God of revelations, but their "I," insisting on complete attention.

In the course of their years of meditation and contemplation, the Elders confronted the most fundamental and deepest aspects of the human condition. Long before the disciplines and breakthroughs of psychology or neurology, these men and women identified states of mind that they termed "the afflictions," and which, in outline, resemble what in popular culture are called the Seven Deadly Sins.

In response to the assaults of desire for food, sex, and material possessions; anger and dejection; *acedia*, vainglory, and pride, the Elders developed highly sophisticated and profound antidotes for these conditions, without recourse to altering their states of consciousness through meditation or drugs or a combination of both. Their immensely practical teachings provide specific methods for dealing with inner thoughts, emotions, and passions when they arise, based on a radical honesty about our human condition.

The wisdom of the Elders couldn't have opened up to me at a more opportune moment. I'd returned from Bolivia ill but, nonetheless, with enormous zeal. I'd met God and undergone a trial that had changed me and enkindled me from within. Unlike my experience at CUA, where my encounter with religious texts had been mostly exegetical, concerned with morality and doctrine, these monastic sources were intensely personal and deeply grounded.

Benedict's great insight was that the work of the monastery was not simply about men and women living apart from society in a community. The true work lay in how one developed the interior life, and how the monastic forms—the hours of prayer, the chanting of the psalms, the life of community, the things we held in common, the obedience, and the silence—rounded out the day and encouraged strength of purpose for that disciplined life. These forms existed to foster that commitment to our vows and were what kept us faithful to this inner work.

Benedict saw that, without the inner work, the monastery is just another worldly institution, vulnerable to the abuses of power and personal and perspectival drift that occur when an organization loses its original genetic moment and its members no longer grasp, or stay focused on, its essential mission.

When I became prioress, one of my most satisfying tasks was working with grant money from the Lilly Endowment to examine the status and direction of women's monastic communities. Our entire community reached back into the foundational sources to retrieve, reclaim, and reappropriate monasticism for our times. We studied and produced our own breviary (composing the seven volumes of the Divine Office). We re-examined our vow of poverty and accepted the new option of taking the vow of total renunciation, which cuts off the option of keeping any inheritance money as an individual.

We learned how to finance a community such as ours through our own ordinary income and raising funds from outside sources for capital improvements. We closed several of our outlying mission houses and brought home the "mission sisters" to Beech Grove. We shifted our mission from the parish to the monastic community, recognizing that the monastic way of life *was* the mission, and by living it faithfully and holding all things in common we presented an ongoing conversion of striving to be a community loving God above all accomplishments. Our training in prayer in common was enhanced through training in prayer as individual nuns employing meditation and *lectio divina* (the personal, prayerful reading of scripture).

A mission of prayer and hospitality challenged the recent history of an emphasis within monastic life on education and monastic-sponsored institutions. In many ways, what we were doing was countercultural, since the dominant trend in religious life was to move out of collective living and into small groups that worked with the marginal and the poor. Religious sisters felt called to live in the midst of alienated, underserved persons. By returning to the idea of "seeking God" under a Rule and an abbot, we were retrieving the original vision of St. Benedict.

During my eight years of administration, our monastery took great strides toward living more contemplatively, something that required a critical mass of sisters residing at the mother house. Even though the economic necessities of feeding and caring for members and listening to compelling calls to do apostolic outreach may be part of the monastic world, a commitment to silence, the cloister, the cell, and monastic observances are the real work of the Benedictine monastery.

For me personally, this work completed the circle of research and study that had been left undone when I was a novice and a student at Catholic University. As a group we studied our monastic sources and aligned our prayer life and governance to be in congruence with our tradition.

Both Benedict and the Desert Elders recognized that even a religious experience such as the one I'd had beneath the river would not sustain me for a lifetime, precisely because I was also the same weak creature who required God's mercy and succor on the mudflats. Even with an increased appreciation of the monastic code and discipline, and my gradual awakening to the under-the-river teachings contained in Benedict's sources, I knew that, without the inner work suggested by the *Rule* and the Elders, my own propensities and the surface and sub-surface flotsam and jetsam that washed down the interior river with me would continue to remain more life-threatening and destructive than the physical flood in Bolivia.

It became very clear that what I needed was not to return to "normal," which would in effect mean continuing to allow emotional and relational debris to pile up on the shore of my life. I needed to dive deep into the spiritual life, without getting the psychic "bends" or losing my consciousness and drowning, and the *Rule* was the diving bell that would allow me to explore the depths in safety. I needed to cultivate Benedict's purity of heart—a state of grace where you are free of judgment, and your mind, body, and soul are at peace, and all relationships are ordered toward the one relationship with God.

Because I've written four other books that explore in great detail the application of the practical skills and spiritual insights of the Desert Elders, I won't go deeply into this wonderful tradition here. It's enough to say that I was enabled by the grace of God for the most part to retrain my thinking patterns, thought by thought. I could only learn this restructuring of consciousness by doing it. It required me to wait upon the impulse of the Holy Spirit so I'd know what was directed toward God and not my created thoughts about the self, so I could trust and thus discover what *truly* was my heart's desire.

In essence, I realized I had to watch my inner thoughts at every moment. It wasn't enough to recite the psalms in choir practice; I needed to observe my mind and attend to the subtle presence of God while I prayed with the other nuns, or by myself in my cell. This in turn meant making sure that I didn't confuse my core identity with my thoughts and emotions. They could rise and vanish and not touch my inner self. I had to redirect all my deeds and achievements, and my emotions and grievances, toward God, remaining vigilant for those subtle tones of self-aggrandizement that add discordant notes to the harmony of the soul.

None of this was, or is, easy. But it's the necessary inner work of a monastery—beyond the external, common life of manual labor, prayers in chapel, and ministry to the Church. Over the course of the years, I've found that by constantly reorienting myself toward God, rather as I angled my body toward the mudflats in the Rio Roche, I can gain some sanctuary from the inner flood. In some ways, it's the truest gift I can return to the selflessness of Oscar and Raul, who risked their lives for me.

◄-◄-►-►

Since my intense engagement two decades ago with the wisdom tradition that lay behind the *Rule of Benedict*, the afflictions have begun to disperse, at least from time to time, and have been replaced by a deeper sense of God's presence. They haven't vanished. Sometimes they wash over me with vast and bewildering force; and for stretches at a time I feel relief, only for the flood to return with so much strength that I'm helpless to swim against its forces.

Simply living in a convent hasn't made me safe from my interior flood, or stopped me from obsessing on my own thoughts and feelings. But the practices mean I can lessen the length of time the afflictions last, weaken the impact they may have on my soul, and reduce the damage I may do to myself or others through acting on the impulses stirred up by the afflictions. I've become better at discerning their onset and on rare occasions have even been able to shift myself toward God—that place where all feelings, thoughts, and desires sit back and rest and there's no fuel for destructive or heightened emotions.

Working with the wisdom of the Elders hasn't been the only practical method that I've employed over the years to help me transform the afflictions into a kind of tool for disciplining the mind and an alarm clock to wake me up from any complacency I may have. I've sometimes found it useful to engage a spiritual elder and disclose to her what I'm experiencing so that the mental poison, as it were, is extracted from me. This isn't simple talk therapy, but two spiritual practitioners praying to God for help and mercy to help discern a way to leap the obstacle that hides the joy of monastic life.

As in that night in Bolivia, I've also been rescued by the psalms. They remind me that, while I'm made in God's image, I'm nevertheless utterly dependent on God's grace. Likewise, just as at no point in the litany of woes that the psalmist lays before the Creator is the Creator's reality ever in doubt—for even the terror of being forsaken by God depends on there being a God to feel abandoned by—neither is the profound vulnerability of the human creature ever forgotten.

Like all prayers or statements from human beings, the psalms are not intended to explain why some individuals are persecuted and suffer while others appear blessed and fortunate. What the psalms *do* provide is a powerful connection to the reality of the human condition. Both my experience underneath the river in the gentle, white light and seeing the strikes of lightning on the mudflats—counterindicative though they may seem to be—were equally valuable and equally true, and both were equally my experience of being a creature before the divine.

The psalms remain an extraordinary gift, as fresh and alive to me as they were twenty-five years ago, and every week before and since. I can live behind the eyes of the psalmist and identify with the writer's vulnerability and desperation, the fear and terror, the joy and petulance, the gloating over one's enemies and fantasies of revenge.

Nowadays, I prefer those moments when I simply, softly chant the psalms one after the other in choir, day after day. The direct tones of the music and the cadence of the words are a continuous blessing. Usually, they sing through me like they did that night in Bolivia. In this, I'm not only connected to those moments a quarter of a century ago, but even to a conversation I had or email I read a few minutes prior. I return over and over again to the original sentiments of the psalmist: joy and agony, grief and exultation, bewilderment and loss, and being without shelter. Although we chant them in the comfort of the monastery, the psalms are at work in me as if I'm still sitting on that mud relief in the Rio Roche.

In all I've done—whether in my work in interreligious dialogue or my attempts to absorb wholly the wisdom of the Desert Elders—my goal has been to dive from the surface and plumb the depths in search of the silence that is the presence of God. I have realized that thoughts—the inner stuff that flows downstream with us—*matter*. They matter because, unless we are careful, they sweep away our true selves. When I *watch* these feelings arise, and try to do so without inner commentary, most of them simply dissolve and go away. The larger task is to guard my heart so those thoughts don't get inside of me in the first place.

One question I hear from others who know the story of

what happened to me, Juanito, and the three nuns is whether I'm healed yet. I understand the compassion and concern (as well as, perhaps, the impatience) behind this inquiry; however, it misses the point. Far from wanting to be healed from the memories of what happened, I seek to hold fast to the pain and loss, as well as the intimacy and terror, of the deaths, the rescue, and the reception by the nuns at the back door of Our Lady of Grace. God's fierce attention is nothing I want to "get over."

Indeed, as much as I found peace of heart at that Easter Vigil in St. Louis in 1969, or in that glance toward the shrine at Catholic University in 1983, so I have wanted to look into the face of terror. Unlike the clinical depression or the dread I felt, terror felt to me at once less abiding and sharper. It stripped me of my own illusions. Furthermore, although such fearful intimacy continues to overload my emotions on occasions, I nonetheless consider it a privilege to be so wholly known by God—to have met, as it were, face to face—and to abide in a place of truth that, while raw and naked and deeply revelatory of my own abiding weakness, is entirely *real*.

Consequently, my true desire is not to be "healed." I don't want to flee the human condition or dissolve into mindlessness. When I was asked beneath the river whether I wanted to die, the response of *not now* was as significant as the *no* itself. The *not now* was a way of saying that life as I know it *does* end, but that I didn't choose it to end at that moment.

In the consent to life, as I know it now, was also my consent to die, at least physically. I count on that same saving grace to guide me when I face death again.

Furthermore, although I felt great fear and desperation that night, and came face to face with both the deep reservoir of my desire to live and my profound powerlessness in trying to dictate the terms of my survival, I no longer fear death, because I've seen something of what death is and also what life beyond death looks like. I know that we're invited to the next life with grace and poise.

Death is not simply a cessation of breath; it's a journey to someplace else. Although I can't determine the exact nature of the realm after death, I do know it is beautiful and serene. God extends a personal invitation—whether we ask for it or not—that affirms that we're not merely the result of a random molecular fusion, an accident of time and space that's of no consequence either before or after our time on this planet. We are inspirited beings, subject, to be sure, to the weaknesses of the flesh, but loved and cherished in our totality. We are loved as particular souls and unique persons. Who would want to "get over" this?

Beneath the river that night in Bolivia I met a personal God who knew me and whom I'd already known. I could count on God's mercy with no fear. Above the river, on the mudflat in the Rio Roche, I also encountered a personal God who was terribly present. In fact, far from crying into an empty void, there was nothing to protect me *from* God. I was wholly seen by God in the lightning and thunder. It was clear to me that I was nothing and God was everything, and it was wholly appropriate to kneel, bend low, and adore the Creator.

It may be hard for some to resolve in their minds the paradox of these experiences, but to me they are facets of the same *tremendum*—the earth-shaking voice of God and the still, small voice of calm that are our encounters with the inescapable. When confronted by the force of God's creation and one's nakedness within it, all that one can do is place one's head on the wet earth and pray with all of your might for help.

Some mystics have reported that their encounter with God led to a union with the divine or a deep understanding of God. This was not my experience. I'm no closer to uniting or being with God than I was before that night in Bolivia; I'm a desperate creature in need of God's mercy. I have none of the ability to talk or think "about" God found in the theological books and journals, and most speculation about God's nature feels haughty and blasphemous to me.

That night in Bolivia, I never felt more mortal, or so aware of my need for salvation. It's an awareness I've never lost. Because I knew I couldn't have survived by my will alone, or even through the assistance of other people, but only through God, I felt my precariousness as keenly as I responded to my own rescue. In other words, every day I recognize that I've been saved, and every day I know how much I need to be saved.

It is for these reasons that I don't want to banish the reality of the afflictions, just as much as I never want to forget or to numb either the peace I felt beneath the river or lose that wholesome fear of the Lord. The afflictions from which I suffer are a consequence of a lack of discrimination or because I do not possess the skills to train and stabilize my mind. I have needed to renounce my former life over and over, and accept that I only want one relationship—my avowed and celibate one with Christ.

I've seen others step away from this commitment, and although for others the commitment may have shifted into a new outer form, to leave the monastic way of life isn't an option for me. My commitment is not to some ideal, such as being a nun for the sake of being a nun. It's rather to give attention to my mind, thoughts, and emotions. It's in this narrow path of one relationship, one monastic way of life, and one undivided heart that I've found freedom from chaos and complexity. The older I get, the more satisfaction I gain by staying focused, resisting other options, and letting go of systems that say I can have it all. The One is quite enough.

9

Returning to Christ

The relaxing of the afflictions is only half of the story these last twenty-five years. The other half concerns the deepening comfort and attraction I find in the God who had a face, who had emotions like mine, who was present to my mind's eye at the instant of attention, and who makes all questions irrelevant: Jesus Christ. When the afflictions relax and Jesus replaces anger, depression, and pride, I, naturally, without effort, go back to my childhood love of him, my first experience of religious life, and with my public vows as a nun. My heart's desire returns with a felt love, such as that sense that I was known under the Rio Roche.

What is Jesus to me? He's the man of the Gospels—the distinctive individual who sits at the table with others, who walks with believers on the road to Emmaus, who suffers alongside criminals on the cross, and who prays to his father in the Garden of Gethsemane. Even though, of course, Jesus' historical physical body is not with me, his subtle body is, and he helps to direct my observations and allows me to see my own blind spots. He guides me gently away from being overly judgmental or distracted by something that would harm or would take me away from the public vows I've made. The face of Jesus dissolves the kind of fear that hurts and replaces it with a loving glance.

I am not Jesus, nor has he merged into my consciousness. Our relationship is much as a couple that has taken vows of marriage yet are still two people although they've joined together to form "one body." This language might be shocking or strange to contemporary ears; but these spousal images have nothing to do with our common assumptions or notions about gender. The relationship is sacramental and known by the subtle senses beyond any sexual or erotic connotations.

In this relationship with Jesus, I've no illusions about being special or sainted or holy, for everyone has the opportunity on the Christian path to seek God. Jesus is my partner in colloquy. To my silent questions he replies either in the form of a voice in my head that I hear as clearly as my own, or his words appear on the page when writing. Through these techniques, and the recitation of the Jesus Prayer—"Lord Jesus Christ, son of the living God, have mercy on me, a sinner"—I am centered once again in my heart's desire. When the afflictions arise or my heart grows tepid and cold, I simply return to my practice with concerted effort. Sometimes I don't feel the presence of Christ, but I always feel the presence of faith, which has a sweetness all its own and is enough for me.

When circumstances cause me to lose that equanimity, or take me back to the great vulnerability I felt on the mudflats of the Rio Roche, I fly for refuge into the wounds of Jesus on the cross. This symbol is akin to the psalmist pleading for safety in a crevice in a cliff face. I find comfort kneeling before a crucifix that depicts Jesus' suffering on the cross. He, too, drew on the psalms in his moment of agony—"My God, my God, why have you forsaken me?" (Matthew 27:46).

The wounds are an expression of human feeling: that it is as if God cries out when I do, that Our Lord no more likes hunger or desperation, confusion or agitation, than any of us. God was present at the death of the three nuns and Juanito. These wounds aren't salved with easy promises or protestations of loyalty, but instead focal points for the reality of that agony. I'm not commanded to be tougher and grit out my distress; it's not my task to reach for ease. I'm asked, instead, to concentrate on Jesus' wounds and let the afflictions pass through my consciousness. The cross is the stable place for an aching heart.

This is my practice even when I don't feel the afflictions, for I'd only be fooling myself if I believed that anger, dejection, vainglory, and whatever else may cover over my consciousness of Christ, won't return, and do so in strength. I must also keep turning away from the ego and its language—not to obsess over my failures and incompleteness but to bow and ask for God's mercy. I have to release any agenda I may have for achieving a higher state or personal development, or even happiness. A deeper contentment no longer allures me. The raw experience of the human in me is fine the way it is.

And here is perhaps the most profound connection between the devotion I have for Christ and the experience I had that night in Bolivia. What Christ suffered, the physical pain I underwent, and the afflictions that cloud my life aren't to be closed off or covered over, but used as openings to grace. I don't mean self-inflicted pain, which stems from a pathology that deliberately seeks attention or pride in suffering. Instead, I mean the bearing of the wounds that allow growth, like rings in the core of a tree or knots that report the emergence of a branch.

No one weeps more than God when we make choices that reject grace to do otherwise and come to decisions that feed violence and destruction. We may be made in the image of God, but our likeness is still malleable. Poor creatures though we may be, we cannot understand the larger picture of which we are a tiny part, but through our wounds we're given a glimpse of the abiding presence of God's mercy wherein healing saturates fear and anxiety with love.

Every day, I pass by our oratory in the novitiate wing

of Our Lady of Grace Monastery where the life-sized form of Jesus is carved on a beautiful oaken cross. Reaching just above my head, I can place my fingers in his wounded side. I see this gesture not as a fetish or superstition, but a prostration—an act of humility that in its simplicity is echoed in many religious traditions, and in its own way recalls the old woman's taking hold of my hand more than a quarter of a century ago. In her woundedness and mine, she reaches out for me; when I place my fingers on the cross, through Jesus's suffering and dignity, I feel her fingers touching mine. I hear Gilchrist's laughter, and see Juanito's two thumbs lifted in pleasure, and through them I join with the suffering and dignity of all creatures under God.

My relationship with Jesus changes every day and is always renewed. In this way, I exist wholly within the Christian tradition, although I recognize the force and majesty of other faith practices, and their many authentic revelations of God. Jesus is the way and truth and life for me; yet I know that in God's wide wisdom there are many ways toward what I experience as God. Not only have I been privileged to come to know very holy persons who are as committed to their faith as I am to mine, but the God I encountered beneath the river didn't ask whether I was Jewish, Muslim, or Christian, but only let me know that I was loved and known.

When I become caught up in apologetics, proselytizing, or any other form of trying to lay my vision over somebody else's, it seems like my old competitive agenda emerging again. Of course, it's easy to write it, but the cunning forms of besting others are always a temptation. That's why I value dialogue so much; it's a wonderful way to contribute to the work of the Church without any agenda of evangelization that intends to convert the other.

Because of dialogue, I've been blessed with many moments of grace working with people from other faith traditions. In 1995, for instance, I traveled to the foothills of the Himalayas in northern India and then into Tibet as part of a group representing Monastic Interreligious Dialogue. In the highest places, where ancient temples are still active shrines, I performed the ritual circumambulation of the *stupas*.

Far removed from the Christian symbols I was used to, I found myself filled with the simple words of the Jesus Prayer—a call from the depths like the psalms that night in 1984. This time, however, the prayer wasn't a plea for safety or rescue, but an expression of desire to rest in the love of God's mercy. The Jesus prayer fell with the same cadence as the chants of the pilgrims who arrived at this holy site through many rugged, narrow passes. We were praying together and yet apart.

◄◄--►►

When I think back over the course of my life, I realize

I've always been on a quest to understand the meaning of "vocation," a word that comes from the Latin *vocare*, to call. A "calling" is not a job or even one's work. It's a summons that emerges from a desire so deep that it cannot be rationalized by the conscious mind. Indeed, as those reluctant prophets Moses and Jonah discovered, God's invitations can be deeply inconvenient and sometimes terrifying. Jonah was so disturbed by what he was being asked to do that he fled, even to be swallowed whole by a great fish. But as Jonah discovered, no matter how inadequate or unprepared or scared you may feel yourself to be, God will always find you and point you in the right direction.

As the lives of Gilchrist and Rita, Gerry and Mary attest, American women religious have an outstanding history of professional service, and they continue rightly to challenge policies that exclude women from liturgical life and high positions in the institutional Church. But, more importantly, my apostolic sisters remind all of us of our duty toward the least and the underserved. My community is known for our zeal. Our hospitality is ever at work on behalf of others; and our liturgy, especially the Divine Office, is outstanding thanks to wonderful musicians and poised liturgical ministers.

The challenge that now faces communities such as mine is that there aren't enough hours in the day to meet the demands of professional ministering and comply with Benedict's original vision of being in community and practicing the contemplative life. Like the team in Bolivia, from time to time we need to discern what our mission is and refocus on it accordingly.

Until recently, I grappled with what it meant to be a nun. I've come to see that there are many authentic ways to live the monastic life. Some do not take the vow of stability; some have no community. I know that my particular vocation has some elements that are non-negotiable; but I can acknowledge that others may have their own particular directives. I've lived the monastic life with my Benedictine community in Beech Grove for fifty years—as a student, a novice, superior, and now an elder. I assume that I'll be buried there in God's time. However, while I value deeply my membership in the community, it's my relationship with God that I treasure most. And as I grow older, I find myself more deeply drawn to silence and the cloister, more convinced than ever that the special gift of the Benedictine monastic life should be as rigorous in training for the inner life as we study for years for our outer lives as professional ministers.

When I look back at the young lifeguard who, at seventeen, had joined the Benedictines, I see a youth full of zeal and a novice with high ideals. My turbulent formation program, my years as a grade-school teacher, my academic training that could have led to living in an apartment some place as a professor to some university, and my years in catechetical administration for the Archdiocese of Indianapolis—all left me with a split between how to live the monastic way of life and work in the world. It's one that continues to challenge me to this day.

Nonetheless, I have always been clear as to my vocation and my orientation toward God. As I near a half century of living with my vows, I increasingly have a sense of the impulse of grace taking me where I need to be. I know that whatever reforms may be necessary for living an authentic monastic life, the first and deepest change must start with me. By the grace of God I am alive, and grateful beyond words, with an abiding and wholesome fear of God.

Epilogue
Return to Charamoco

In January 2009, I accepted an invitation to return to Bolivia to commemorate the twenty-fifth anniversary of the deaths of Gilchrist, Mary, and Gerry, and little Juanito. I had been back to Bolivia since the accident. In 1986, as the superior of Our Lady of Grace Monastery, I'd made a formal visitation to our missioners in Cali, Colombia, and had then traveled on to Bolivia, where I was made an honorary member of the village of Charamoco. On that occasion I met Oscar and Raul, who'd literally saved my life two years previously. Twenty-three years later, I'd initially been uncertain about whether to return to Bolivia, but Rita assured me I'd be welcomed by the Maryknoll Sisters at Casa Rosario (two of whom I'd known twenty-five years ago), and so I decided to go. The journey would also give me a wonderful opportunity to visit my brother Jim and my sister-in-law Marina, who now live in La Paz.

As it turned out, I arrived a week after the official memorial service, where a Mass was said by Father Matt Mueller and celebrated by a delegation of Dominicans and Maryknoll missioners. Because we took public transportation, my guide, Maryknoll Sister Margaret Smith, and I never made it to Charamoco to see what had changed nor did we meet any of the rescue party, including Oscar or Raul. Nevertheless, the people I met were as warm and generous as I remembered them; the Church's priests and sisters continued to play a major role in everyone's lives; and every January the community came together for a Mass for the dead.

That January day, Sister Margaret and I did manage to walk toward the river where I'd experienced such terror and serenity. In the full sunlight of a warm summer day, I was struck once again by the scale of the topography that lay before me. The river depression between the mountains appeared to me to be a good two miles from bank to bank, and even though it wasn't in flood, it was easy to see how powerful the Rio Roche could become should the tributaries merge and the *acequias* overflow and the water come cascading down into the valley.

The mountains that flanked the Rio Roche rose beyond the steep banks that, since 1984, had been marked by a new, larger road carved into their sides, and which carried great earth-moving trucks hauling ore mined from the mountains near Capinota. A new bridge crossed the river. Yet in spite of these efforts by human beings to bend the natural world to our will, everything man-made still seemed small compared to the majestic height of the mountains and the expanse of the river: the huge trucks I saw moving slowly along the road seemed mere toys in comparison with the terrain.

I noticed, etched into the sides of the canyon, the waterlines left by previous floods, perhaps even more devastating than the one that carried me and took the lives of the nuns and Juanito. Around me, the pampas grass grew luxuriantly. Cows were tethered to trees scattered among the tilled soil of cornfields. By the positioning of the trees around the opening of the river into the valley, I could see that the flood of 1984 must have risen to the level of the treetops for me to be slammed into the branches.

As I stared out at the river before me, I placed my hand on the altar erected to honor the three nuns and the little boy and I recited my vows to God once again. I had brought with me my soprano (descant) recorder and I played two tunes: "Amazing Grace" and "The Rose." I also wore a watch like the one Juanito liked to remove and put back on my wrist. I took it off and placed it beneath the sideways cross representing Juanito, which supports the three upright crosses that connote Mary, Gerry, and Gilchrist. Then, after an hour or so of sitting and praying in silence, Sister Margaret and I walked back up to the main road, hailed a passing taxi filled with other passengers, and hitched a ride back to Charamoco.

About Mary Margaret Funk

Mary Margaret ("Meg") Funk, OSB, has been a member of Our Lady of Grace Monastery at Beech Grove, Indiana since 1961. She taught elementary school at St. Barnabas 1965–69, and she was an administrator for the Archdiocese of Indianapolis in catechetics from 1969 to 1983. She also was Coordinator for Adult Religious Education (1984–85) for the Archdiocese of Louisville.

From 1985 to 1993, she was Prioress of Our Lady of Grace Monastery, and in 1994 became Executive Director of the board of Monastic Interreligious Dialogue. In that capacity she coordinated two Gethsemani Encounters (1996 and 2002), and two Benedict's Dharma conferences (2001 and 2003). She spoke at the World's Parliament of Religions in 1993, traveled to India and Tibet on the Sixth Spiritual Exchange Program in 1995 and 1999, and has been in formal dialogue with Hindu, Zen Buddhist, Islamic, Confucian, and Taoist traditions.

The author of several books on John Cassian and the Desert Fathers and Mothers, Meg has given many retreats to monastics and lay ministers on Christian practice. She served on Thomas Keating's Contemplative Outreach Board of Trustees; Weston School of Theology in Cambridge, Massachusetts; and was a member of the Board of Overseers of St. Meinrad School of Theology. She holds graduate degrees from Catholic University of America (1973) and Indiana University (1979). She's a graduate of Epiphany Certification Program of Formative Spirituality (2002).

Of Related Interest from Lantern Books

THE SPIRITUAL LIFE
A Dialogue of Buddhist and Christian Monastics
Edited by James Wiseman and Donald Mitchell
978-1-59056-173-7

FINDING PEACE IN TROUBLED TIMES
Buddhist and Christian Monastics on Transforming Suffering
Edited by James Wiseman and Donald Mitchell
978-1-59056-172-0

GREEN MONASTICISM
A Buddhist–Catholic Response to an Environmental Calamity
Edited by William Skudlarek and Donald Mitchell
978-1-59056-167-6

THE COMMON HEART
An Experience of Interreligious Dialogue
Edited by Netanel Miles-Yepez
Foreword by Ken Wilber
1-59056-099-X

Of Related Interest from Lantern Books

GOD'S HARP STRING
The Life and Legacy of the Benedictine Monk, Swami
Abhishiktananda
Edited by William Skudlarek
978-1-59056-167-6

WHEN GOD SAYS NO
The Mystery of Suffering and the Dynamics of Prayer
Daniel Lanahan
1-930051-90-5

THE TENDER HEART
A Buddhist Response to Suffering
Ven. Yifa
978-1-59056-111-9

THE TRANSFORMATION OF SUFFERING
Reflections on September 11 and the Wedding Feast at Cana in
Galilee
Thomas Keating
1-59056-036-1